The Somatic Path

The Body's Quiet Intelligence for Wholeness

Jim Daunt

ISBN: 978-1-0699772-0-5

Table of Contents

Introduction

How the Body Releases Separation and Remembers Oneness

Awakening is often spoken of as a moment of insight, a flash of realization, a shift in perception. But real awakening — the kind that transforms your life, your presence, your capacity, and the way you move through the world — does not happen in the mind.

It happens in the body. It happens in the nervous system. It happens in sensation. It happens in breath. It happens in the places where you brace, tighten, shrink, protect, disconnect, or go numb.

Awakening becomes real only when the body begins to release the contraction it has been holding since the moment you first learned to separate yourself from the world, from others, and from your own deeper truth.

This book is about the path the mind cannot walk — the body's path to awakening.

Awakening Is Somatic — And It's Also Practical

Although this book is deeply spiritual, it is equally **practical**. Because the same contraction that blocks your spiritual awakening also blocks:

- your capacity for intimacy

- your ability to receive wealth
- your resilience under pressure
- your clarity in decision-making
- your expression of purpose
- your access to pleasure, joy, and creativity
- your physical health and vitality

In other words: The body doesn't just hold separation from the Divine. It holds separation from life.

And until contraction softens, all areas of your life feel restricted. This is why people who are brilliant, capable, spiritually aware, and deeply insightful still struggle in:

- relationships
- finances
- self-worth
- confidence
- emotional regulation
- leadership
- intimacy
- creative expression

It is not because they lack mindset, discipline, skill, or spiritual insight. It is because their nervous system is still wired for survival, not expansion.

This book will show you why somatic awakening is not just a spiritual path — it is the foundation of **living fully, loving**

deeply, receiving generously, and succeeding without self-betrayal.

The Body Stores Separation

Every moment of tightening, every freeze response, every breath you held, every time you braced against life, every time you felt alone, unseen, or unsupported — the body recorded it. Not as memory. But as **identity**.

Separation is not just a mental illusion. It is a **somatic pattern**, a physiological contraction, a nervous system strategy, a survival posture. The ego is not just a set of thoughts — it is the **shape your body took** when it didn't feel safe.

Awakening requires healing this shape. Personal success requires rewiring this shape. Relationships require softening this shape. Abundance requires expanding this shape.

The body became the first place the ego lived. And the body must become the first place it unwinds.

Awakening Is Not Leaving the Body — It Is Returning to It

Many seekers attempt to awaken by transcending:

- pain
- emotion
- desire
- the body
- the world

But true awakening moves deeper **into** your experience, not away from it. You awaken by:

- feeling what you once avoided
- softening where you once braced
- allowing what you once suppressed
- breathing where you once froze
- staying present where you once disappeared

The body is not the obstacle to awakening — it is the doorway. And beyond spirituality, the body is also the doorway to:

- clearer thinking
- emotional intelligence
- deeper intuition
- clean decision-making
- embodied confidence
- healthy boundaries
- attracting aligned relationships
- creating abundance without contraction

This book will show you why somatic liberation is the foundation of **all forms of success**.

Awareness Heals by Becoming the Space Around Sensation

When you shift into the observer — the witnessing presence — something extraordinary happens:

- sensation can move
- emotion can release
- tension can unwind
- fear can soften
- identity can loosen

Awareness doesn't heal by forcing change; awareness heals by **holding what arises without collapsing into it.** This is where your spiritual path intersects your personal path. The more awareness you bring into the body, the more capacity you gain in every domain of life. Because:

- the regulated nervous system leads better
- the open heart receives more
- the grounded body thinks more clearly
- the soft belly allows creativity
- the calm breath reveals intuition
- the coherent field attracts abundance

Your spiritual awakening becomes the engine of your personal growth.

Divine Co-Regulation: The Missing Link in Both Awakening and Success

Human nervous systems do not heal in isolation — they heal through connection, support, and presence. This is true spiritually **and** practically. When you feel connected to something greater than the ego, the body releases layers of fear that block:

- emotional intimacy
- wealth and opportunity
- authentic self-expression
- intuitive clarity
- healthy boundaries
- creativity and purpose

Spiritual connection is not separate from your worldly success. It is the **foundation** of it. Because the nervous system can only expand into greater responsibility, visibility, receiving, or intimacy when it feels held, supported, and safe.

This book will show you how divine co-regulation is not just a mystical truth — it is a **performance advantage**, a **healing accelerator**, and a **magnetic field for abundance and aligned relationships.**

Intimacy, Receiving, and the Nervous System

Nothing reveals your level of consciousness and somatic openness like intimacy and receiving. You may consciously desire:

- love
- wealth
- respect
- connection
- pleasure
- purpose

- opportunity

But your nervous system may not yet feel **safe** to hold them. This is why many people:

- sabotage success
- collapse under pressure
- fear visibility
- struggle to receive love
- avoid intimacy
- overspend or undercharge
- reject compliments
- push away support
- tighten around money

These are not psychological weaknesses. They are somatic contractions around receiving. And when these contractions soften, your entire life expands.

The End of Separation Is the Beginning of Embodiment

As the body releases old survival patterns, something extraordinary happens:

- health improves
- relationships deepen
- boundaries strengthen
- financial flow stabilizes

- intuition sharpens
- creativity awakens
- confidence becomes natural
- love becomes effortless
- purpose feels obvious
- life becomes lighter
- awareness becomes embodied

This is not a spiritual bypass. This is spiritual embodiment.

And it is also **personal growth at the highest level** — because you stop living as a fragmented, defended, survival-driven identity and begin living as a grounded, connected, receptive, coherent human being.

This Book Is an Invitation:

- to wake up spiritually
- to grow personally
- to receive deeply
- to succeed cleanly
- to love fully
- to live in coherence
- to embody unity

It is an invitation to let your life expand at the same rate your body soften, and at the same rate awareness enters your contractions. It is an invitation to remember:

Your spiritual awakening is not separate from your health, your wealth, your relationships, or your fulfillment. They are all expressions of the same inner transformation: the body releasing separation and returning to Oneness.

Welcome to The Somatic Path to Awakening. Your body has been waiting for you.

I

The Body as the Gateway to Awakening

Chapter

1

The Forgotten Truth: Awakening Is Somatic

Awakening as a Whole-Body Remembering

Awakening is not something the mind achieves. It is something the body remembers.

Long before we learn to talk about spirituality, the body has already been speaking. It speaks in contraction and expansion, in breath and holding, in the subtle micro-movements of fear and the effortless openness of safety. Awakening begins the moment we realize these somatic signatures are not obstacles to enlightenment but the very doorway into it. The body is not something we transcend on the way to higher consciousness — it is the terrain through which higher consciousness becomes real.

There is a forgotten truth at the heart of awakening: **the body is the first place separation was ever felt**, and so it is also the first place unity must be rediscovered. Before the mind formed language, beliefs, or identity, the nervous system learned what was safe, what was dangerous, what could be received, and what needed to be braced against. These early somatic impressions became the scaffolding for our sense of self. In other words, the body remembered separation long before the mind explained it.

And so awakening is not the acquisition of new ideas — it is the unraveling of old contractions. It is the softening of the physiological patterns that taught us to hold ourselves apart from life, from others, and from our own Presence. When people speak of awakening as "coming home," they are describing this return: the dissolving of the inner bracing that once kept us small, defended, or divided.

This is why awakening cannot be forced through thought. Thought can point us toward truth, but it cannot deliver us into it. Insight alone may clarify the path, but only embodiment transforms it. The mind may recognize oneness conceptually, yet the body must feel safe enough to let that recognition permeate. Without somatic release, awakening remains an idea — beautiful, inspiring, but disembodied. When the body relaxes, however, the boundary we call "self" begins to loosen, and a deeper intelligence emerges — one that is ancient, instinctive, and inherently whole.

This whole-body remembering is not dramatic. It often unfolds in quiet moments: the soft exhale after a lifetime of holding; the unexpected ease that moves through the chest when resistance drops; the subtle widening of perception when the nervous system stops anticipating danger. These are the micro-awakenings that accumulate into the greater awakening. Each one is the body saying, *I remember. I remember what it is to trust. I remember what it is to open. I remember what it is to belong.*

Awakening, then, is not an ascent but a descent — a dropping back into the body, into sensation, into the intelligence that was always here. It is the recognition that consciousness does not merely reside in the mind but pulses through muscle, fascia, and breath. It is the realization that every tension held in the body was a fragment of self trying to protect us, and every release is a fragment returning home.

When this remembering deepens, awakening becomes unmistakably somatic. The body begins to reorganize around truth, not fear. Breathing becomes easier. Emotions move more freely. Presence replaces vigilance. And life itself begins to feel less like something we must survive and more like something we are continuously emerging into.

This is the forgotten truth: **Awakening is not an escape from the body — it is the body's liberation.** And as the body softens, what returns is not something new but something ancient: the felt knowing that we were never truly separate, never truly alone, and never truly disconnected from the field of consciousness that holds everything.

Awakening is the body remembering what the mind forgot: *Oneness was never lost.*

Why the Mind Cannot Awaken Alone

The mind is brilliant at creating reflections of truth, but it cannot become truth. It can articulate insights, map out pathways, and form exquisite structures of understanding, yet it cannot cross the threshold into awakening by itself. Awakening is not a cognitive event — it is a shift in being. And being lives in the body.

The mind can glimpse awakening the way someone standing outside a home can glimpse the warm glow through the window. But it is the body that opens the door and walks inside.

We often assume that if we stack enough insights, read enough teachings, or master enough concepts, awakening will naturally follow. But intellectual clarity is not the same as somatic freedom. You can understand everything about surrender while the body remains braced. You can speak about oneness eloquently while the chest is tight, the belly is clenched, and the nervous system is still living in separation. You can know the truth yet still feel profoundly divided inside. That is because the mind interprets reality, but the body stores reality.

The mind cannot transcend what the body continues to hold. If the nervous system is contracted, awakening remains partial — an idea floating above an untransformed physiology. And ideas, no matter how profound, cannot release the freeze in the diaphragm, unwind decades of survival tension, or dissolve the subtle vigilance that shapes perception at a deeper level than thought could ever reach.

Awakening fails to stabilize when the mind tries to carry it alone, because the mind can only shift narratives, while awakening requires the shifting of capacity. True surrender is not a belief but a physical letting go. True openness is not an attitude but a state of the nervous system. True presence is not attention but coherence. Without these somatic shifts, "awakening" becomes a mental performance — clear on the surface yet fractured underneath.

This is why certain people develop what could be called "floating awakening" — a state where the mind is awake to truth, but the body has never caught up. They speak in non-dual language, yet they still struggle with reactivity, fear, need for control, and the subtle ways the ego hides in the nervous system. Their awakening lives above the neck.

Chapter 1

The mind cannot unwind its own illusions because many of its illusions are somatically reinforced. The ego is not just a psychological structure; it is a physiological configuration — patterns of breath, muscle tension, hormonal cascades, survival impulses, and conditioned responses. The mind cannot dismantle what it did not build. The ego lives as much in the tissue as in the thought.

When the body is left out of the awakening process, the mind attempts to awaken while still being tethered to the physiological patterns of separation. It tries to transcend what the body continues to defend against. It tries to "let go" while the nervous system remains braced. It tries to "be present" while the physiology remains primed for threat.

This is the quiet frustration behind so many seekers' journeys: the sense of "I understand this, so why can't I live it?" The answer is simple: the mind understood, but the body did not yet feel safe enough to follow.

Awakening stabilizes only when the body joins the remembering. When the breath softens, when the chest opens, when the old contractions loosen, when the survival responses unwind — then the mind is no longer carrying awakening alone. Awareness begins to permeate the whole system. Presence drops from concept into embodiment. Knowing dissolves into being.

And in that shift, awakening stops being something we chase with the mind and becomes something that unfolds through the body — naturally, inevitably, and without force. The mind cannot awaken alone because awakening is not a thought. It is the return of the whole self into coherence, wholeness, and truth.

How Separation Shows Up in the Nervous System

Separation is not an abstract metaphysical concept. It is a lived, biological experience — felt first in the nervous system long before it becomes a belief, a story, or a philosophy about who we think we are. The nervous system is the body's memory of separation. It holds the imprints of every moment we contracted, every moment we felt unsafe, every moment life registered as "too much," "too fast," or "not allowed." These somatic impressions form the foundation of ego long before the mind ever names it.

To understand how separation arises, we must look not at thought, but at physiology. The nervous system is constantly scanning for danger, constantly evaluating its own capacity, constantly determining whether openness is safe. When the system perceives threat — real or imagined — it narrows. Breath shortens. Muscles tighten. Awareness collapses inward. In these moments, we don't merely feel separate from the world; we become structurally organized around separation. Survival is a somatic contraction, and that contraction becomes the body's template for "self."

Most people believe their sense of "I" is mental, but the first version of "I" is somatic. It is the body tightening around an experience and interpreting that tightening as "me." When the chest constricts, the diaphragm freezes, or the belly hardens, the nervous system creates a boundary — not the healthy boundary of discernment, but the survival boundary that says, I must hold myself apart to stay safe. This is the origin point of separation. It begins in sensation, not thought.

Over time, these patterns become familiar. The nervous system repeats what it knows. If our early environment taught the body that openness leads to pain, the system contracts long before the mind is aware of why. If connection felt unpredictable, the system stays vigilant even in moments of love. If expressing emotion once caused overwhelm or rejection, the system learns to numb instead of feel. These physiological adaptations eventually solidify into personality, identity, and the subtle sense that we are alone inside ourselves.

Separation shows up as bracing — an invisible holding pattern in the shoulders, jaw, pelvis, or breath. It shows up as numbness — a disconnect from sensation that was once too much to process. It shows up as hypervigilance — the subtle leaning forward into life, anticipating what might go wrong. It shows up as collapse — the sinking inward when the system feels powerless. These are not psychological tendencies; they are survival responses etched into tissue.

The mind later builds stories to explain what the body already decided. "I'm not enough." "I need to be perfect." "I must stay in control." "I can't trust others." But these beliefs are the mind's interpretation of much deeper somatic truths: "I don't feel safe." "I don't have capacity." "I am braced against experience." "I am protecting myself from overwhelm." The ego is simply the mental narrative layered on top of the body's command: Stay separate so you can survive.

This is why awakening cannot bypass the nervous system. If the physiology is still operating from separation, the mind may have moments of clarity, but the lived experience remains fractured. You can intellectually understand unity while your body still moves through the world as if danger is everywhere. You can glimpse oneness in meditation but return to old patterns the moment the nervous system is triggered. When the body is anchored in survival, the mind's awakening is temporary.

The moment the nervous system begins to regulate, soften, and expand, something profound happens: separation no longer feels necessary. The body discovers that openness does not threaten it. The survival impulse eases. The bracing unwinds. The vigilant scanning quiets. And in that softening, the boundary between "self" and "life" becomes permeable. Presence expands outward. Awareness becomes less local. The sense of being separate dissolves not because we forced it to, but because the body is no longer holding itself apart.

Separation was never purely psychological; it was physiological. And awakening is not the mind remembering truth — it is the nervous system remembering safety. When the body relaxes, unity becomes inevitable. The return to oneness is not a mental insight but a lived, somatic unfolding.

The Illusion of "Mental Awakening" Without Embodiment

One of the most subtle traps on the spiritual path is the illusion that awakening can be achieved through understanding alone. The mind is so quick, so capable, so hungry for clarity that it can easily convince itself it has arrived somewhere the body has not yet followed. It collects insights, adopts language, synthesizes teachings, and creates a beautiful internal map of truth. But maps are not landscapes. And the mind's awakening is not the awakening of the whole being.

"Mental awakening" is the illusion of arrival without the lived transformation that makes awakening real.

It looks like clarity without freedom, insight without ease, wisdom without regulation. It sounds coherent, but it feels tight.

It speaks about non-duality, presence, surrender, and unity, yet the nervous system quietly remains in contraction. The breath is still shallow. The body is still braced. The emotional field is still guarded. There is still a subtle layer of vigilance woven through the system. The mind may have adopted the language of truth, but the body is still living in the frequency of separation.

This form of awakening floats above the surface of life. It hovers in concepts, philosophies, and high-level perspectives. There is an elegance to it, and often a seductive clarity. But because it is disembodied, it cannot anchor into the deeper layers where the ego actually resides — layers made of sensation, tension, memory, and survival reflex. Mental awakening rearranges belief, but it does not unwind the musculature of fear. It refines perception but does not soften the diaphragm. It expands perspective but does not expand capacity.

This is why many people experience a dissonance on the path:

- they know they are not separate, yet they feel profoundly separate
- they understand surrender, yet cannot let go
- they speak of presence, yet still react from old wounds
- they grasp unity, yet still brace against intimacy, emotion, or uncertainty

This is not failure. It is simply the recognition that awakening cannot remain an intellectual event. The nervous system must participate.

The ego, after all, is not merely a mental structure — it is a somatic one. It lives in the subtle tightening around identity, the freezing around vulnerability, the bracing around emotional risk. If these patterns remain untouched, the mind can proclaim awakening while the body continues to hold the imprint of separation. This creates a divided state: spiritually expansive above the neck and somatically constricted below it.

From the outside, "mental awakening" can appear luminous. But internally, it is fragile, easily disrupted, and dependent on controlled environments. One moment of overwhelm, one difficult relationship, one unexpected emotional trigger, and the entire mental structure collapses back into familiar survival physiology. That is because the mind was never the one holding the awakening — it was simply holding the idea of it.

Embodied awakening feels different. It is grounded, spacious, and deeply human. It is humble and unforced. It is not trying to transcend the body but to inhabit it fully. Its stability comes not from conclusions but from coherence — breath, awareness, presence, and nervous system safety working in tandem. This kind of awakening does not shatter under pressure because it is not dependent on mental control. It lives in the tissues. It breathes through the heart. It moves through sensation.

Mental awakening without embodiment is like sunlight without warmth. It illuminates, but it does not melt what needs to be softened.

Only when insight descends into the body — when the nervous system relaxes, when emotional contractions unwind, when breath becomes unguarded — does awakening become whole. The illusion of mental awakening dissolves, and what remains is something real, integrated, and unshakable: a state of consciousness lived through the full human instrument, not just imagined by the mind.

Chapter 1

What It Means to Awaken Through Sensation Rather Than Thought

Awakening does not happen in the mind — it happens in the felt field of the body. It happens in the moment you stop trying to understand your experience and begin to feel it. It happens when sensation becomes the gateway, not the obstacle. Awakening through sensation is the shift from interpreting life to directly experiencing it. It is the movement from thinking about truth to embodying it.

Most people try to awaken through the intellect because thinking feels safer than feeling. Thought gives us distance, control, and the illusion of mastery. But sensation asks for something deeper: vulnerability, presence, and surrender. Sensation cannot be managed or manipulated in the same way thought can. It must be met. It must be allowed. It must be felt without negotiation. This is why sensation is the truest path to awakening: it bypasses the mind's defences and touches the very place where separation was stored.

When you awaken through sensation, you stop chasing transcendence and begin dissolving contraction. You stop seeking answers and begin meeting the inner landscape exactly as it is. You stop trying to "fix" yourself and begin allowing the body to reveal its own intelligence. Sensation becomes the teacher. Awareness becomes the witness. And the nervous system becomes the pathway home.

Awakening through sensation means noticing the tightness in the chest not as a problem, but as a doorway. It means meeting the trembling in the belly without trying to calm it prematurely. It means allowing the heat, the pressure, the buzzing, the numbness, the pulsing, the ache — all the subtle textures of experience that the mind once avoided or controlled. Each sensation is a fragment of yourself asking to be integrated. Each one is an unopened letter from your past, offering its wisdom the moment you stop resisting it.

As you rest in sensation, something extraordinary happens: the body begins to reorganize around truth. Tension unwinds. Old emotional residues surface and complete. The survival reflex loses its grip. Breath deepens without effort. Presence expands from the inside out. You begin to experience yourself not as a thinker of thoughts but as the space in which sensation arises. And the moment you recognize yourself as the space, the boundary between "self" and "experience" begins to dissolve.

This is the somatic unfolding of awakening: the realization that you are not the tension but the awareness that holds it. Not the fear but the field in which fear moves. Not the story but the spaciousness beneath it. Sensation becomes the bridge between the conditioned self and the unconditioned truth of who you are.

Awakening through thought is linear, structured, and limited by language. Awakening through sensation is spacious, organic, and rooted in direct experience.

Thought can only describe what sensation reveals. Sensation, on the other hand, speaks in the original language of the nervous system — one that predates belief, identity, or personal history. When you stay with sensation long enough, it begins to reveal the places where the body still remembers separation. And as those places open, soften, and release, awakening slowly descends out of theory and becomes embodied reality.

To awaken through sensation is to let the body participate fully in your evolution. It is to let awareness touch the exact places where you once tightened against life. It is to discover that truth is not something you grasp but something you feel — a lived resonance that emerges when the inner holding dissolves. This is the heart of somatic awakening: truth realized not in thought, but in the warm, open depth of a body no longer braced against itself or the world.

The Gateway You've Always Carried

Awakening is not something the mind achieves — it is something the whole being remembers. When we return to the body, we return to the place where separation was first felt and where unity is ultimately restored. What we often mistake as spiritual progress has, for many, been a journey of accumulating insights rather than dissolving contractions. Yet the truth is simple: awakening stabilizes only when the nervous system becomes a safe place to receive life.

The mind can point toward truth, but it cannot embody it. The body is where awakening becomes real. It is here, in the shifting of breath, the unwinding of tension, the softening of long-held contraction, that consciousness descends out of philosophy and becomes lived experience. Every moment of presence that meets sensation without resistance is a moment of returning. Each opening is a recalibration of the entire system — an exhale into a deeper truth than the mind alone can access.

As we embrace this somatic path, awakening stops being a pursuit and becomes a process of remembering — remembering the safety beneath survival patterns, the openness beneath fear, the clarity beneath mental complexity, and the unity beneath the illusion of separateness. We discover that awakening is not found “above” life but through it; not beyond the body, but intimately within it.

The forgotten truth is that the body has never been an obstacle to awakening. It has always been the gateway. And as you move forward, the path will not ask you to transcend your humanity but to inhabit it more fully. The more you feel, the more you release. The more you release, the more you open. And the more you open, the more awakening becomes not a moment of insight but a living, breathing state of coherence.

This chapter ends where the real journey begins: with the profound recognition that awakening is somatic, and the body is ready to lead you home.

Chapter

2

How the Body Holds Separation

Duality as a Somatic Experience

Duality is not born in the mind — it is born in the body. Long before we develop language, philosophy, or belief systems, the nervous system is already organizing the world into categories: safe or unsafe, pleasant or overwhelming, open or closed. This primal sorting becomes the body's first experience of duality, and it lays the foundation for how we later perceive ourselves, others, and reality itself.

Duality is not originally a concept of "me" and "not me." It is a physiological distinction between what my system can stay open to and what my system must defend against. The moment the nervous system contracts, tightens, or goes into bracing, duality appears — not as a thought, but as a felt split. It is the body saying, Here is where I end and the world begins. Here is where I must hold myself apart.

This split is subtle, almost invisible in daily life. A tightening in the chest when someone raises their voice. A clenching in the belly when uncertainty arises. The micro-frozen quality in the diaphragm when an emotion approaches that once felt too big to process. These are not random sensations; they are the somatic traces of duality. They are the body enforcing a boundary that once served survival.

As we grow, the mind builds stories around these contractions — stories about identity, worthiness, capability, and control. But beneath every story is the same somatic truth: the body learned to divide experience in order to protect itself. What spirituality often calls "separation" or "ego" is, at its root, the body remembering where it once felt overwhelmed.

Duality persists because the nervous system continues to operate as if the past is still happening. It abbreviates life into categories. It narrows around what feels familiar. It guards against openness because openness once felt dangerous. Even the simplest contraction in the body becomes a small version of duality — an inner "no" that interrupts the natural flow of presence.

This is why awakening cannot be merely a shift in perspective. The perspective may change, but if the body still contracts in the same ways, duality remains alive within us. Unity cannot be felt through a nervous system that is bracing; oneness cannot be lived through a body still holding the imprint of danger.

Duality dissolves not when the mind understands non-duality, but when the body no longer needs to separate itself from experience. When the chest softens instead of tightening, when the breath stays open in the face of emotion, when the belly no longer clenches in anticipation of threat — something remarkable begins to occur. The boundary that once felt fixed begins to blur. Presence expands. The sense of self becomes less localized. Awareness starts to include, rather than exclude, the world.

In this way, duality is revealed for what it truly is: a somatic adaptation, not an existential truth. The body created it to survive, but the body can also release it. And when it does, we begin to feel what the mind could only conceptualize — an unguarded, unseparated openness that is the first embodied taste of awakening.

Childhood Imprinting and Survival Physiology

Before we learn language, before we form memory, before we have any sense of "self," the body has already learned how to survive. Childhood is not merely a psychological formation period — it is a somatic one. The nervous system, still tender and unguarded, absorbs every tone of voice, every moment of attunement or misattunement, every silence, every burst of tension in the room. These early experiences do not become stories; they become physiology.

A child's body learns the world long before the mind understands it. If the environment is warm, responsive, and emotionally coherent, the body learns openness. Breath flows naturally. Muscles rest. Sensation is allowed. The child's system encodes safety as the baseline for existence. But if the environment is unpredictable, chaotic, withdrawn, or demanding beyond the child's capacity, the nervous system adapts by contracting. It tightens, freezes, or becomes hypervigilant. The child learns to survive through bracing.

These early adaptations become imprinted as the body's "truth" — not intellectual truth, but somatic truth. The child does not think, I'm unsafe. The body decides it. The child does not reason, I must hold myself together. The nervous system does it automatically. These physiological patterns form the architecture of the ego long before the mind ever constructs identity.

Every unmet emotional need becomes a signal to the nervous system: Open here, close there. Lean forward. Pull back. Stay small. Stay quiet. Stay alert. The body organizes around whatever kept the child protected. What begins as a momentary adaptation becomes, over time, a habitual way of being.

Many adults live from these childhood imprints without realizing their origin. The tightness in the throat when speaking up. The sinking in the belly when someone is disappointed. The rigid posture of always anticipating the next demand. The inability to fully relax, even in moments of safety. These are not personality traits — they are survival physiology echoing from a time when the body had no other option.

The mind later builds narratives to justify these imprints:

- "I'm shy."
- "I'm anxious."
- "I just don't like conflict."
- "I have trouble trusting people."

But beneath these narratives live the original somatic truths:

- "I once needed to withdraw to feel safe."
- "I once had to scan constantly to predict danger."
- "I once had to silence myself to avoid overwhelm."
- "I once had to carry tension to hold myself together."

The body remembers what the mind forgets.

These imprints also become the foundation for the illusion of separation. When the body repeatedly experiences moments of overwhelm, neglect, or emotional dissonance, it learns that connection is not inherently safe. It learns to create an inner divide — a buffer between itself and life. What spirituality later describes as the "ego" is, in its earliest form, nothing more than the body managing too much sensation with too little support.

Awakening begins when we stop judging these patterns and begin understanding them. Every contraction in the adult body was once a child's act of intelligence. Every bracing pattern was once an attempt to preserve a fragile sense of self. These imprints are not failures; they are proof that the body did everything it could to survive.

And because they were learned, they can be unlearned — not by force, but by meeting the body with the safety it never had. When awareness enters these old patterns with compassion rather than judgment, the nervous system begins to revise its original conclusions. The body learns that what once required contraction can now be experienced with openness.

Childhood imprinting formed the architecture of separation. Somatic awakening is the gentle, patient unraveling of it.

The Ego's Contraction: Bracing, Tightening, Numbing

The ego is not just a psychological pattern; it is a physical posture. It lives in the body as contraction — subtle, chronic, and often invisible to the one living inside it. While the mind narrates the story of "I," the body enforces it through bracing, tightening, and numbing. These three forms of contraction are the ego's somatic architecture, the way the nervous system maintains the illusion of a separate self.

Bracing is the body's quiet attempt to stay ahead of life. It is the subtle forward lean of vigilance, the tightening around the heart that anticipates impact, the shoulders lifting ever so slightly as if protecting against an unseen blow. Bracing says, "Something could happen at any moment, and I must be ready." It is the nervous system's way of holding the world at a distance, preparing for a threat that may no longer exist. Most people live in a perpetual state of micro-bracing, unaware that this constant readiness is the foundation of their suffering.

Tightening is the body's effort to contain what feels unmanageable. It shows up in the clenched jaw, the rigid spine, the gripping belly, the held breath. It is the nervous system's instinctive response to overwhelm: If I contract around this, maybe I can control it. Tightening creates the illusion of stability, but it also restricts emotion, intuition, and presence. It is the body's attempt to control life by reducing its fluidity. In tightening, the ego forms its boundaries — not the boundaries of healthy discernment, but the boundaries of fear.

Numbing is the ego's last line of defence. When bracing and tightening are no longer enough, the body learns to mute sensation altogether. Numbing is not absence — it is suppression. It is the body saying, I cannot feel this and still survive, so I will not feel it at all. This can take the form of physical numbness, emotional blunting, dissociation, or a muted sense of aliveness. Numbing is the ego's way of preserving coherence by shrinking the range of experience the system will allow.

Together, bracing, tightening, and numbing create the somatic cocoon that the ego mistakes for "self." These contractions shape our perception, limit our capacity, and distort our sense of what is possible. They make the world seem sharper, heavier, more threatening. They shrink our ability to receive support, joy, intimacy, or abundance. And because they operate below conscious awareness, they often feel like reality rather than a survival response.

This is why purely mental or philosophical approaches to awakening fail to dissolve the ego. The ego does not live in thought — it lives in tissue. You cannot reason your way out of a clenched diaphragm. You cannot affirm your way out of a frozen belly. You cannot meditate your way past numbness if the nervous system has not yet learned that feeling is safe.

As these contractions dissolve, the ego's structure begins to soften. Bracing gives way to presence. Tightening gives way to flow. Numbing gives way to sensation and emotional truth. The sense of "I" becomes less rigid, less defended, less reactive. Awareness begins to permeate the body, not just the mind. And in this softening, awakening moves out of theory and into lived experience.

The ego's contraction was never a flaw — it was an intelligent adaptation to an overwhelming world. But it is no longer needed. As the nervous system learns safety, the body no longer has to hold itself apart. The somatic shell of ego dissolves, and what remains is openness — unbounded, undefended, and naturally aligned with truth.

The Freeze State as the Physical Form of Separation

Among all the survival responses, freeze is the one most deeply tied to the illusion of separation. Fight mobilizes energy. Flight redirects it. But freeze suspends it. It is the nervous system's last resort — a moment when the body determines that neither resistance nor escape is possible, and so it withdraws inward. In that withdrawal, we experience the most profound somatic expression of "I am alone."

Freeze is not stillness. It is immobilization. It is not peace. It is disconnection. And yet, to the untrained inner eye, freeze can masquerade as calm, neutrality, or even spiritual detachment. In truth, it is the body shutting down to protect itself from overwhelm, intensity, or threat. It is separation encoded into physiology.

When the body enters freeze, sensation becomes muted or distant. The breath becomes shallow or barely perceptible. Emotions feel locked behind an invisible wall. Awareness narrows. The world feels far away. It is as if consciousness retreats into a small, protected chamber inside the body — one the mind later mistakes for a "self."

This inward collapse forms one of the earliest templates for the ego: I must separate from life to survive. Freeze teaches the body that separation equals safety. It teaches the nervous system that contact — whether emotional, relational, or sensory — is too much to handle. Over time, this internal withdrawal becomes a familiar refuge, a physiological identity: the quiet, contained version of you that learned to disappear in order to stay intact.

Adults rarely notice their freeze states because they feel normal. A muted sense of aliveness. A difficulty accessing emotion. A tendency to go blank when conflict or intimacy arises. The subtle "checking out" during moments of vulnerability. These experiences do not appear dramatic, but somatically, they are profound: the body is pulling consciousness inward, creating a divide between the self and the world.

Freeze is the physical embodiment of separation. It is the body's declaration: I cannot be here. I cannot feel this. I cannot stay open.

And yet, this state often gets misinterpreted as spiritual progress. People mistake numbness for equanimity, emotional distance for detachment, dissociation for transcendence. But awakening does not come from leaving the body — it comes from returning to it. A body in freeze cannot awaken because awakening requires presence, and presence cannot coexist with withdrawal.

The path out of freeze is not force but safety. Not trying to "push through," but learning to gently thaw. Thawing is the somatic unwinding of separation — the slow return of sensation, breath, emotion, and relational contact. It is the body discovering that it is no longer in danger, that it can re-enter the world without being overwhelmed. Thawing is not always graceful. Sometimes sensation rushes back like a flood. Sometimes it returns in tiny waves. But each moment of thaw is a moment of reconnection.

As freeze melts, something unexpected occurs: the sense of isolation dissolves. The body begins to feel part of life again. Awareness expands outward instead of collapsing inward. Emotion becomes fluid rather than contained. The nervous system reorganizes around openness instead of withdrawal.

This thawing is not merely emotional healing — it is spiritual awakening. Because the moment the body no longer needs to separate from experience, the illusion of separation itself begins to collapse. And what emerges in its place is the natural state the body always knew before survival interrupted it: a direct, unguarded participation in reality. Presence. Connection. Oneness.

Why Unprocessed Emotions Keep Identity Intact

Identity is not held together by belief — it is held together by unprocessed emotion. The emotions we could not feel, could not express, or could not metabolize in childhood became the building blocks of the ego. They were too overwhelming for the young nervous system to experience fully, so the body learned to contain them. That containment — those pockets of held emotion — became the scaffolding of the separate self.

Unprocessed emotions don't simply disappear. They remain stored in the body as tension, bracing, numbness, or chronic activation. And because the mind cannot tolerate open loops of unresolved experience, it constructs narratives around these sensations. It creates meanings, identities, and roles to make sense of the emotional weight the body continues to carry. In this way, identity forms around what has not yet been felt.

- Fear becomes "I'm cautious."
- Rejection becomes "I'm not enough."
- Shame becomes "I need to be perfect."
- Abandonment becomes "I must stay independent."
- Anger becomes "I have to stay in control."

Each identity is not a truth but a strategy — an adaptation to an emotion the system was not safe enough to process when it first emerged.

The ego remains intact because these unresolved emotions remain intact. They are the glue that holds the separate self together. When an emotion rises toward the surface — toward completion — the ego feels threatened, not because the feeling itself is dangerous, but because the dissolution of that emotional imprint would unravel a piece of its identity. The ego is not afraid of emotion; it is afraid of losing the structure emotion created.

This is why awakening requires a descent into sensation. You cannot release the ego by thinking through it. You must meet the emotional contractions that gave it form. And yet, the mind often resists this process. It prefers clarity over feeling, interpretation over embodiment. But the body knows the truth: the only way to dissolve the identity built on emotion is to feel what was once unfelt.

Unprocessed emotions also maintain the illusion of separation because they keep the system in a constant state of partial threat. A body holding fear sees the world as dangerous. A body holding shame feels fundamentally flawed. A body holding grief perceives life as loss. These emotional imprints shape perception, not because the world is inherently threatening, but because the nervous system is still protecting a younger version of us who once felt overwhelmed.

When emotions finally move — when they are allowed to arise, complete, and release — the identity built upon them begins to soften. The narratives lose their charge. The boundaries that once felt like survival begin to dissolve. A new spaciousness opens inside the system. What once felt like “me” now feels like sensation passing through awareness.

As unprocessed emotions unwind, the body becomes less defended, the mind becomes less reactive, and the sense of self becomes more fluid. You begin to feel the difference between who you truly are and who you became in response to what you could not feel. This is the beginning of true freedom — the freedom that arises not from transcending emotion but from liberating it.

Identity dissolves in direct proportion to how much of the emotional body is brought back into awareness. When nothing is being held, nothing is being defended. And when nothing is defended, separation cannot sustain itself. The body returns to coherence, the heart returns to openness, and the self returns to spaciousness.

Unprocessed emotion created the separate self. Fully felt emotion dissolves it.

Where Separation Was Stored, Wholeness Begins

Separation did not begin as a belief — it began as a bodily response. It lived first as contraction, overwhelm, and the instinctive maneuvers the nervous system used to survive what it could not yet process. The stories we later told about who we are were built on top of these somatic truths. The ego formed not from thought but from the body's early attempts to stay safe, to stay connected, to stay intact.

As we've seen throughout this chapter, the body holds separation in many forms: the duality imprinted in childhood, the subtle bracing of the ego, the numbing that once protected us from feeling too much, the freeze that turned presence into distance, and the unprocessed emotions that became the foundation of identity. These patterns were never mistakes —

they were intelligent adaptations. They were the body's way of saying, I'm doing everything I can to keep you alive.

Awakening begins the moment we stop fighting these patterns and start listening to them. The moment we understand that separation is not a spiritual flaw but a physiological imprint. The moment we realize that the body is not resisting awakening — it is waiting for enough safety to release what it has been holding for years, decades, or even a lifetime.

When we bring awareness to these contractions without judgment, something shifts. The body slowly learns that it no longer needs to brace. Sensation becomes less threatening. Emotion becomes less overwhelming. Presence becomes less conditional. And the boundary between the self and life begins to soften. Separation dissolves not because we transcend the body, but because we finally enter it.

This chapter closes with a simple but profound recognition: Everything that once held you separate lives in the body, and everything that will return you to wholeness begins there as well.

As you move into the next chapter, you will begin to see how the ego and the nervous system co-create the illusion of danger — and how awakening unfolds through the unraveling of that very loop. The path ahead is not upward or outward but inward — toward the body's deepest intelligence, its capacity for safety, and its innate orientation toward unity.

Chapter

3

The Nervous System and the Ego

The Ego as a Protective Physiological Pattern

The ego is not born in the mind. It is sculpted in the body. Long before the mind forms concepts of "I," the nervous system has already created a physiological pattern whose sole purpose is protection. What we later call "ego" is simply the mental interpretation of a much deeper, older survival mechanism — one that originates in sensation, not thought.

The ego begins as the body's instinctive response to overwhelm. When a child encounters more intensity than their system can process — emotion, conflict, absence, unpredictability — the nervous system contracts to maintain coherence. That contraction, that attempt to hold the self together, becomes the earliest seed of ego. The body tightens, narrows, withdraws, or braces, and the mind eventually builds an identity around these states. The story of "me" grows from the body's attempt to stay safe.

This is why the ego feels so personal. It lives in our breath, our posture, the space behind our eyes, the clutch in our stomach, the tension in our shoulders. It is woven into the subtle ways we hold ourselves separate from life. The ego is not an enemy — it is a physiological strategy that once ensured our survival. It is the body saying, Let me protect you from what felt too overwhelming to feel.

As we grow, this protective pattern becomes habitual. The nervous system repeatedly chooses contraction over openness, vigilance over presence, control over trust — because these strategies worked at one time. The ego solidifies not because we are flawed, but because the body remembers. It remembers the moments when openness felt dangerous. It remembers the overwhelm that made shutting down feel necessary. It remembers how shrinking, pleasing, performing, withdrawing, or hardening helped us navigate a world we had no power to change.

The mind then takes this physiological foundation and creates a narrative around it: This is who I am. This is how I must be. This is what it takes to survive. But underneath every identity is a somatic truth: the ego was formed in response to a body that felt alone in its experience.

Understanding the ego as physiological shifts everything. It frees us from the belief that awakening requires defeating the ego or dismantling it through force. You cannot fight a protective pattern into submission. You can only help the body feel safe enough to release it. The ego softens not through insight but through regulation. It dissolves not through will but through the gradual unwinding of contraction.

When the body learns that it no longer needs to brace, the ego naturally loosens. When the nervous system feels supported, the sense of separation begins to fade. When the physiology experiences safety, the identity built on fear and defence no longer makes sense. Awakening happens not because we transcend the ego, but because the nervous system no longer requires it.

The ego was never the obstacle — it was the body's best attempt at love. And as awareness meets this pattern with compassion rather than resistance, the protective layers begin to fall away. What remains is not a diminished self, but a truer one — unarmored, uncontracted, and available to the fullness of life.

Why Trauma Equals Somatic Identity

Trauma does not just shape memory — it shapes identity. Not because of what happened, but because of what the body had to become in order to survive it. Trauma is not the event itself; it is the imprint that the event leaves on the nervous system. It is the contraction, the bracing, the shutting down, the vigilance, the numbing, the tightening that the body adopts as a strategy for enduring what it could not otherwise process. Over time, these survival patterns harden into a sense of self. They become me.

This is why trauma equals somatic identity: the body's adaptations to overwhelm become the blueprint for who we believe we are.

When an experience exceeds the nervous system's capacity, the body reorganizes itself around safety. The breath changes. Muscles constrict. Awareness narrows. Emotion becomes fragmented or inaccessible. The body learns to inhabit smaller spaces inside itself, to avoid certain sensations, to brace against specific relational cues, to stay alert for signals that resemble earlier overwhelm. These physiological adaptations become familiar. They become home. And the mind begins to interpret them as personality.

- A child who learned to disappear in moments of intensity becomes the adult who identifies as quiet or invisible.
- A child who learned to stay hyper-attuned to others becomes the adult who identifies as empathic or responsible.
- A child who learned to numb their emotional field becomes the adult who identifies as "logical" or "unaffected."
- A child who learned to contain anger becomes the adult who identifies as calm or compliant.

None of these are identity — they are survival strategies the body practiced long enough to feel like self.

Trauma becomes identity because the body encodes the adaptations as necessary. The nervous system concludes:

- this is how we stay safe
- this is how we avoid pain
- this is how we stay connected
- this is how we keep from breaking

And once the body believes this, the mind begins creating beliefs to match. Thought follows physiology, not the other way around. The stories of "who I am" arise from the somatic patterns underneath them.

Trauma is not just remembered; it is embodied. It becomes the tension in the chest, the guardedness in the heart, the vigilance behind the eyes, the heaviness in the limbs, the holding in the gut. These patterns generate emotional pathways, behavioural tendencies, and relational dynamics that reinforce the illusion of a fixed self.

This is why spiritual insight alone cannot dissolve identity. Identity is not mental — it is physiological. And until the nervous system feels safe enough to release the patterns formed in trauma, the stories built around those patterns remain intact. Awakening will feel partial, inconsistent, or out of reach, not because we lack understanding, but because the body is still organized around survival.

When the somatic imprint of trauma begins to soften — when tension unwinds, when emotion moves, when breath deepens, when vigilance relaxes — the sense of self shifts in ways thought cannot orchestrate. Suddenly the identity we once defended begins to feel foreign, unnecessary, or too small to inhabit. The old "me" loses its solidity because the physiology that maintained it is dissolving.

This is the heart of somatic awakening: You do not lose yourself. You lose the version of yourself the body created to survive. Trauma becomes identity when the body has no other choice. Identity dissolves when the body finally feels safe enough to let go.

The Nervous System's Primary Directive: Survival, Not Truth

The nervous system is designed for one purpose: to keep you alive. Not fulfilled, not peaceful, not awakened — alive. Every perception, reaction, and contraction in the body is rooted in this primary directive. The nervous system evaluates the world not through the lens of truth, but through the lens of safety. It does not ask, Is this real? It asks, Is this safe? And whatever is deemed unsafe becomes filtered, distorted, or avoided entirely.

This is why awakening does not come naturally to the unregulated system. Truth often requires openness, vulnerability, stillness, and surrender — states the nervous system may interpret as threatening if it was conditioned to survive through tension, vigilance, or control. The body does not seek truth; it seeks familiarity. And familiarity is often woven from old patterns of contraction.

When the nervous system perceives danger — whether from an external event or an internal sensation — it reacts instantly. Breath shortens. Muscles tighten. Awareness narrows. The mind begins scanning for threat or constructing stories to justify the physiological state. In these moments, we are not perceiving truth; we are perceiving through the filters of survival.

This is why people can intellectually know that a situation is safe while their body reacts as if it is dangerous. The nervous system is not responding to the present moment; it is responding to past patterns, unresolved emotions, and the strategies that once kept us alive. It is not interested in accuracy. It is interested in continuity.

Survival physiology creates a worldview. A nervous system in fight interprets life as conflict. A system in flight perceives life as overwhelming. A system in freeze experiences life as distant or unreal. And a system in fawn perceives life as something to constantly manage through compliance or attunement. These are not conscious choices — they are somatic reflexes. They shape our perception of reality without our permission.

When truth contradicts survival patterns, truth loses. The body will choose contraction over clarity, withdrawal over presence, and control over surrender. This is not dysfunction — it is biology. It is the nervous system doing exactly what it was designed to do.

Awakening requires recognizing this. We cannot shame the body out of survival mode. We cannot force it into openness. We cannot demand that it prioritize truth over safety. The nervous system shifts only when it feels safe enough to do so. Insight alone cannot override physiology. But awareness — gentle, consistent, compassionate awareness — can create the conditions in which safety becomes possible again.

As the nervous system begins to regulate, the body's grip on survival loosens. Breath deepens. Emotion becomes tolerable. Sensation no longer signals danger. Presence expands without resistance. In these states, the body becomes available to truth — not as a concept, but as a lived experience. Truth emerges naturally when the system is no longer defending against life.

In this way, awakening is not the triumph of truth over survival, but the softening of survival so truth can finally be felt. The nervous system will not prioritize awakening — but it will relax into it when it feels safe, supported, and seen.

Safety opens the door. Awareness walks through it. Truth reveals itself.

How the Ego and the Body Co-Create the Illusion of Danger

The illusion of danger — so central to the ego's existence — is not created by the mind alone. It is co-authored by the body. The ego provides the story, and the nervous system provides the evidence. Together, they form a closed loop that convinces us we are threatened when, in truth, we are simply meeting old survival patterns resurfacing in the present.

When the body senses something reminiscent of a past overwhelm — a tone of voice, a facial expression, a moment of uncertainty — it activates an old physiological response. Muscles tighten. Breath shortens. Awareness contracts. The nervous system prepares for impact long before the mind can interpret what is happening. The body reacts first. The story comes second.

And the story always matches the state of the body.

- If the nervous system is braced, the mind interprets the moment as conflict.
- If the nervous system is vigilant, the mind interprets the moment as threat.
- If the nervous system is collapsed, the mind interprets the moment as failure or powerlessness.

These interpretations feel true, but they are simply the mind decoding the body's survival signals. The ego overlays meaning onto physiology and calls it reality.

Meanwhile, the body responds to the mind's interpretations. The more the mind labels a moment as threatening, the more the nervous system contracts. The more the nervous system contracts, the more the mind reinforces the story of danger. This feedback loop becomes self-sustaining: a somatic reaction fuelling a narrative, and a narrative deepening the somatic reaction.

This is how the illusion of danger becomes so convincing. It is not purely cognitive nor purely physiological. It is the fusion of the two — the synchrony of belief and contraction — that makes fear feel absolute.

For example, a person who carries the imprint of childhood rejection will feel a tightening in the body when connection becomes intimate. The nervous system interprets this as impending danger. The ego then creates a narrative: They will leave. I am not enough. Something is wrong. But the body was not responding to the present moment; it was responding to an old memory. And the mind, unaware of the origin, confirms the alarm and strengthens the identity built around it.

Similarly, someone who grew up needing to stay hyper-attuned to others may feel surges of anxiety when things are quiet. The body interprets silence as instability, as if danger is looming. The mind steps in with a story: I must do something. I need to fix this. Something is wrong. Again, the ego interprets somatic data through the lens of past survival.

The ego and the body are not separate; they are partners in maintaining a familiar reality — even if that reality is painful. Both are oriented toward continuity, not truth. Both prefer the known contraction over the unknown openness. Both cling to the illusion of danger because danger once made sense.

Awakening requires breaking this loop — not by fighting the ego or suppressing the body's signals, but by witnessing the entire mechanism with clarity. When awareness notices the pattern — body reacts, mind interprets, body contracts more, mind reinforces — something loosens. The cycle becomes visible. And what is visible can no longer operate unconsciously.

When awareness enters the loop, the nervous system begins to soften. The mind's interpretations lose their authority. The ego's story sounds less convincing. Sensation becomes something to feel, not something to fear. Presence interrupts the old choreography of survival.

In that interruption, truth becomes possible. Not because the ego is defeated, but because the body no longer sustains the illusion of danger. Not because fear is eliminated, but because it is finally seen as memory, not reality.

The illusion dissolves the moment the body no longer collaborates with the ego's protective story. And what replaces it is something the system has long forgotten but never lost: openness, clarity, and the unmistakable sense that life is not against us — it is simply moving through us.

Awakening as the Softening of This Survival Loop

Awakening does not happen through force, effort, or mastery of spiritual concepts. It happens through the gradual softening of the survival loop — the continuous interplay between the nervous system's instinct to protect and the ego's stories that justify that protection. Awakening begins the moment this loop is no longer running our experience automatically.

The survival loop is built on repetition: the body contracts, the ego interprets, the mind reinforces, the body contracts again. This cycle becomes so familiar that it feels like reality itself. Awakening is not a sudden leap into higher consciousness; it is the slow, steady unwinding of this conditioned response. It is the uncovering of the spaciousness that was always beneath the contraction.

Softening does not mean relaxing on command. It means becoming aware of the contraction without resisting it. It means recognizing when the body is bracing and choosing to stay present rather than collapsing into old patterns. It means seeing the ego's narrative not as truth but as a reflection of the body's state. This awareness begins to disrupt the loop, introducing an element that was once missing: choice.

The survival loop operates unconsciously. Awakening brings it into consciousness.

- When we notice the tightening in the chest and offer breath instead of panic, the loop loosens.
- When we feel the impulse to withdraw and instead choose to stay in our body, the loop loosens.
- When we hear the ego's fear-driven interpretation and no longer believe it blindly, the loop loosens.
- When we remain present with an emotion that once overwhelmed us, the loop loosens.

Each moment of presence interrupts the automatic cascade of protection. And with every interruption, the nervous system learns something revolutionary: I can stay open here. I can stay present here. I do not have to contract to be safe. Awakening is the reclaiming of this openness.

As the loop softens, the body begins to discover new options. Instead of bracing, it breathes. Instead of tightening, it expands. Instead of numbing, it feels. Instead of preparing for danger, it rests into presence. The ego, no longer fuelled by physiological alarm, quiets. Its stories lose their urgency. They become background noise rather than the leader of consciousness.

This softening is not a one-time event. It is an ongoing relationship with the body's intelligence. There will be moments when old contractions resurface, because the nervous system is simply revisiting the conditions that once shaped it. But each time we meet these contractions with awareness rather than identification, the loop weakens. The somatic imprint fades. The identity built upon it dissolves.

Eventually, what was once a rigid structure becomes fluid. What was once a defensive posture becomes openness. What was once an unconscious reaction becomes a conscious response. And in this transformation, something profound reveals itself: the self that emerges is not the one shaped by survival, but the one shaped by presence.

Awakening is the nervous system learning that it no longer needs to protect you from life. It is the body discovering that safety and openness can coexist. It is the ego releasing its grip because the body is no longer contracting beneath it.

When the survival loop softens, truth becomes accessible — not as an idea but as a lived state. And in that state, you realize: Awakening was never something you had to achieve. It was something the body had to feel safe enough to allow.

When Protection Becomes Presence

The ego was never the enemy — it was the body's earliest expression of care. Every contraction, every bracing pattern, every moment of vigilance was the nervous system's attempt to shield you from what once felt unbearable. What we later called "identity" or "self" was simply the mind interpreting these physiological strategies. The ego was born from love, not from flaw.

But protection, once essential, eventually becomes limitation. The same patterns that kept us safe in childhood begin to confine us in adulthood. The nervous system continues to respond to life as if the past is still present, and the mind continues to generate stories that justify that response. This is how the illusion of danger takes root — not through logic, but through unexamined somatic memory.

Awakening unfolds when we begin to see this mechanism clearly. When we understand that the ego is not a flaw in consciousness but a reflection of unprocessed experience. When we recognize that our deepest spiritual challenges are not conflicts of belief but expressions of physiology. When we honour that the nervous system is always doing the best it can with the conditions it has known.

As awareness touches these old patterns, protection softens. The nervous system discovers new possibilities. The body begins to trust presence. The ego loosens its grip because it no longer needs to defend against life. What emerges in this softening is not a perfected self, but a truer one — one that can meet reality without distortion, without fear, without the habitual contraction that once defined its existence.

The journey ahead is not about eliminating the ego or transcending the body. It is about bringing the body into such coherence, safety, and openness that the ego's protective architecture naturally dissolves. Presence replaces vigilance. Openness replaces defence. Truth replaces the illusion of danger.

Chapter 3 closes with this essential understanding: Awakening requires not the destruction of the ego, but the liberation of the nervous system. When the body no longer braces against experience, the self that once needed protection dissolves — and the spaciousness of your true nature becomes unmistakably clear.

From here, the path deepens — not into philosophy, but into the somatic mechanics of letting go.

II

Letting Go Through the Body

Chapter

4

The Somatic Mechanics of Letting Go

Letting Go as a Physiological Release, Not a Mental Instruction

Letting go is not something the mind can do on command. It is not a decision, a technique, or a shift in belief. It is a physiological event — a softening, unwinding, dissolving that happens within the body when the nervous system feels safe enough to release what it once held for protection. The mind may want to let go, but the body must allow it.

This is why so many people struggle with the idea of letting go. They try to convince themselves to release fear, shame, hurt, or control through thought alone. They repeat affirmations, adopt new perspectives, or attempt to force surrender through willpower. But thought cannot unwind tension, soften bracing, or dissolve survival patterns. The body cannot be talked out of a contraction it learned through experience. It can only be released through felt safety and embodied presence.

Letting go is a physiological shift, not a cognitive one. When the body finally releases something it has been holding, it is unmistakable. Breath deepens. Heat moves. The chest softens. The belly loosens. The jaw unclenches. Energy that was frozen begins to flow again. Emotion rises and completes its cycle.

Sensation expands rather than contracts. This is letting go — not as a concept, but as a lived transformation.

What we call "holding on" is simply the body maintaining a survival response. A contraction around a moment of overwhelm. A bracing against an emotion that felt too big. A tightening around a belief that once provided safety. Letting go does not mean rejecting these patterns but understanding why they formed — and allowing the body to update its old conclusions.

The mind cannot force this release because the mind did not create the contraction. The nervous system did. And the nervous system only relaxes when it senses that the present moment is safe enough for it to do so. Letting go is less about trying and more about allowing. It is less about effort and more about permission.

Awareness plays a crucial role here. When sensation is met without judgment, when emotion is allowed to move without resistance, when the body is approached with curiosity instead of demand, the nervous system begins to soften. In that softening, the tension that once defined "me" starts to unwind. The memory that once lived in the tissue dissolves. The identity built around protection loses its solidity.

Letting go happens naturally when the body no longer needs to hold on. This is why deepening into presence — not forcing release — is the true path. As we stay with the body, moment by moment, breath by breath, something shifts from within. The body begins to trust. It begins to open. It begins to release without being told to. This is the quiet intelligence of somatic awakening: the body knows how to let go when the conditions are right.

Awakening, in many ways, is the cumulative effect of thousands of these tiny physiological releases. One by one, the contractions fall away. One by one, the places where we once tightened soften. And as the body releases, consciousness expands — not through effort, but through the natural dismantling of all the ways we once held ourselves apart from life.

Letting go is not a task for the mind. It is the body remembering how to relax into truth.

Sensation as the Doorway to Dissolving Identity

Identity does not dissolve through thought — it dissolves through sensation. The mind may describe who we believe ourselves to be, but the body reveals who we have become in response to the experiences we could not process. Every contraction, every knot of tension, every place where the breath stops or the body tightens is a fragment of identity held in physical form. To meet these sensations is to meet the very architecture of the ego.

This is why sensation is the true doorway to letting go: it takes us directly into the places where identity is stored. Identity is not a fixed psychological construct; it is a somatic pattern. It is the accumulation of unresolved emotional impressions, survival responses, and habitual contractions that the body once used to protect us. These patterns form the shape of "me." When we feel into sensation — not resisting, not interpreting, not distracting — we are touching the living imprint of that shape.

Sensation does not lie. It does not deceive. It does not tell stories. It simply reveals the state of the nervous system in this moment: whether we are open or braced, in flow or in freeze, present or defending. This honesty is what makes sensation such a powerful portal. When we come close to the raw immediacy of sensation, we bypass the mind's narratives and enter the truth beneath them.

The dissolution of identity happens in the exact moment we allow sensation to be felt without contracting around it.

- When we feel the tightness in the chest without shrinking away, the story of "I am not safe" begins to lose its power.
- When we feel the heaviness in the belly without resisting, the identity built on fear or shame begins to soften.
- When we feel the trembling, heat, pressure, or numbness without turning it into meaning, the ego's structure loosens.

Identity dissolves not because we intellectually reject it, but because the body no longer supports the contraction that once held it together.

Sensation is the bridge between the conditioned self and the truth beneath it. Each time we stay with sensation rather than escape into thought, we create a moment of intimacy with the deepest layers of our being. We touch the places where the body is still holding the past and give them permission to release. As these sensations unwind, the self we thought we were begins to unravel as well.

This process is not always comfortable. Feeling sensation requires vulnerability — a willingness to let the body speak in a language older than thought. But it is in this direct meeting that the body learns something it could not learn in isolation: *I can feel this and still be safe.* This single recognition, repeated across countless moments, is the engine of somatic awakening.

As sensation is met and released, what remains is not a smaller self but a freer one. A self not defined by contraction. A self not bound by old emotional imprints. A self that has space to breathe, expand, and experience life without the constant overlay of the past.

Sensation dissolves identity because it dissolves the tension that held the identity in place. When the contraction falls away, the “I” shaped by survival falls away with it — and what emerges is the spaciousness of awareness, the truth of who you have always been beneath the holding.

To feel is to free.

How Awareness Transforms Held Tension

Held tension is not just physical; it is emotional, psychological, and energetic. It is the body’s way of storing the past — moments of overwhelm, fear, shame, grief, or confusion that had no room to move when they first arrived. These pockets of tension become frozen chapters of our history, living inside muscle, fascia, breath, and the subtle layers of the nervous system. But tension is not permanent. It softens when it is brought into contact with the one thing it never had at the moment it formed: awareness.

Awareness is not attention. It is not analysis. It is not trying to fix or understand. Awareness is presence — an open, spacious noticing that allows sensation to be as it is. When awareness meets held tension, something begins to shift. The body recognizes it is no longer alone with what it once carried. It recognizes that the conditions are now different than they were at the time of the original contraction. This recognition is what initiates the unwinding.

Awareness transforms tension by giving it what it always needed permission:

- permission to exist
- permission to move
- permission to speak
- permission to release

The mind often approaches tension with resistance: *I don't want to feel this. I need this to go away. There's something wrong here.* This resistance reinforces contraction. But awareness approaches tension with neutrality: *This is here. Let me feel it.* This gentle acceptance shifts the nervous system from a state of defence to one of openness. In that openness, the tension begins to unravel.

Awareness functions like warmth on ice. It doesn't force the melt — it allows it. When we rest our attention in a place of holding, without trying to change it, the body slowly reorganizes around presence rather than fear. The breath deepens. The emotional charge softens. The contraction loosens. What once felt solid begins to flow, ripple, vibrate, or release in waves.

This transformation is not metaphorical — it is biological. When the body feels safe, the parasympathetic system activates, allowing previously trapped survival energy to discharge. Muscles release their grip. Fascia becomes pliable. The freeze in the diaphragm loosens. The nervous system transitions from protection to restoration. Awareness is the catalyst that signals: *It is safe to let go now.*

Awareness transforms tension because it brings coherence to what was once fragmented. It brings connection to what was once isolated. It brings compassion to what was once judged. And in doing so, it gives the body the conditions it needs to complete old cycles of emotion and sensation that were previously interrupted.

As these held patterns unwind, identity begins to shift as well. The stories built around the tension lose their foundation. The beliefs tied to those contractions lose their charge. The reactive patterns that once felt automatic begin to dissolve. This is the somatic nature of awakening: the mind frees itself as the body releases what it once held.

The deeper truth is this: tension does not release because we fight it — it releases because we finally listen to it. Awareness is the listening. Presence is the healer. And the body, once invited into that presence, always knows how to return to its natural state of openness.

When awareness meets tension, the past unwinds, the ego softens, and the doorway to freedom opens from within.

Pendulation, Titration, and Somatic Unfolding

Letting go does not happen all at once. The body does not release in grand, dramatic gestures. It unwinds in waves — small, rhythmic oscillations that allow the nervous system to approach what was once overwhelming without becoming overwhelmed again. This gentle back-and-forth movement is pendulation, and it is one of the core mechanics of true somatic healing and release.

Pendulation is the body's natural rhythm of expansion and contraction, presence and retreat, openness and containment. It is not a sign of instability — it is the sign of a system reorganizing itself safely. When we bring awareness to this movement, we begin to work with the body rather than against it. We stop forcing release and start participating in the unfolding.

The companion to pendulation is titration: the process of feeling only as much sensation as the nervous system can handle in the present moment. Instead of diving into a contraction or an emotion with full intensity, titration invites us to take it in micro-doses. The body learns at a sustainable pace. Sensation enters awareness slowly, piece by piece, giving the nervous system time to integrate what arises.

This is how the body protects us while still allowing us to evolve.

- Pendulation says: You can approach and withdraw.
- Titration says: You can feel a little at a time.
- Together, they say: You can heal without retraumatizing.

Somatic unfolding happens when these principles are honoured. The body reveals itself in layers, not because it is withholding, but because it is wise. Each layer of release prepares the system for the next. Each wave of sensation, each gentle thaw, each subtle loosening is part of a larger rhythm of transformation. When we trust this rhythm, healing no longer feels like a battle — it feels like a remembering.

This process often looks like small shifts: a deeper breath, a wave of warmth, a trembling in the limbs, a spontaneous exhale, tears that surface without story. These seem minor, but they are profound. They are the nervous system completing responses it could not complete at the time of overwhelm. They are the body doing what it was designed to do — resolve, integrate, restore coherence.

Somatic unfolding cannot be forced because the body releases only what it is ready to release. If we try to push too far too fast, the system contracts again, reinforcing old patterns. But when we allow pendulation and titration to guide us, release becomes effortless. The body unwinds naturally, safely, and sometimes beautifully.

This is the paradox of letting go: what feels like slow work is often the deepest work. Each micro-release creates more capacity. Each small opening expands the system's ability to process sensation, emotion, and experience. Over time, the accumulated effect of these subtle shifts is nothing short of transformation. The survival structures dissolve. The identity built on bracing softens. Presence expands.

Somatic unfolding is the body's sacred intelligence in motion. It is the path of healing that happens in harmony with the nervous system, not in opposition to it. It is how the past unwinds itself gently, how protection gives way to openness, and how the body slowly remembers its natural state of fluidity, safety, and wholeness.

This is the real mechanics of letting go: not a sudden leap into freedom, but a rhythmic, embodied unfolding — one tender wave at a time.

Why You Cannot "Think" Your Way Out of Contraction

Contraction is not created in the mind, so it cannot be resolved in the mind. It originates in the body — in the reflexive tightening of muscles, the shallow breath, the collapse of the diaphragm, the bracing of the heart, the freeze in the belly. These responses are physiological, not intellectual. They are the nervous system's attempt to protect you, not a problem for the mind to solve.

We try to think our way out of contraction because thinking gives us a sense of control. The mind believes that if it can analyze the tension, interpret it, explain it, or understand it, the body will follow. But the body does not follow thought — it follows safety. And safety is something the mind alone cannot generate.

Contraction happens when the nervous system perceives threat. No amount of reasoning can convince it otherwise.

- You can tell yourself "I'm safe" while your body is still bracing.
- You can understand the situation logically while your gut remains tight.
- You can repeat affirmations while your chest refuses to open.

The mind may know the truth, but the body remembers the past.

This is why contraction persists even when our beliefs change. The body is not responding to the current moment — it is responding to unresolved experiences stored in sensation, tension, and emotional memory. The mind cannot override these stored imprints any more than it can think its way out of a muscle cramp or a surge of adrenaline. The nervous system releases only when it feels safe enough to do so, not when it is instructed.

Thinking about the contraction often reinforces it. When the mind analyzes a sensation, it pulls us into narrative — stories about why the tension is here, what it means, who is to blame, or how to get rid of it. These narratives tighten the system further because they treat the contraction as a problem rather than a signal. The body then contracts again in response to the mind's interpretation. And the loop continues.

Freedom begins when we stop trying to think our way out and start feeling our way through. The moment we bring awareness to the contraction — without judgment, without fixing, without storytelling — the system starts to shift. Sensation becomes less threatening because it is finally being met. The breath finds its way back into the body. The emotional charge begins to move. The contraction loosens not because we forced it, but because the body recognizes that it no longer needs to protect.

The body does not need intellectual understanding to release — it needs presence.

- Presence communicates safety in a way thought never can.
- Presence allows the nervous system to update its old conclusions.
- Presence softens what effort only tightens.

This is the essence of somatic awakening: release arises not from mental effort but from embodied awareness. When the body is allowed to lead, contraction dissolves in its own timing, through its own intelligence, with a grace the mind could never orchestrate.

You cannot think your way out of contraction because contraction is not a mistake — it is a message. And the moment you stop trying to escape it and begin to listen to it, the body does what it has always wanted to do: let go.

The Body Lets Go When It Feels Seen

Letting go is not an act of force, nor a spiritual achievement, nor the result of intellectual insight. It is the body's natural response when it is finally met with the presence it never had. Everything we explored in this chapter — the physiological nature of release, the role of sensation, the transformative power of awareness, the gentle rhythms of pendulation and titration, and the impossibility of thinking our way out of contraction — points to a singular truth:

The body lets go when it feels seen, not when it is told to. The tension we carry is not random. It is the residue of moments when experience exceeded our capacity. The contractions that shape our identity were formed because they once protected us. They are not obstacles to awakening — they are invitations. Invitations to feel what we could not feel, to meet what we once avoided, and to bring awareness to places that have waited years, or decades, for our attention.

Letting go is not something we do. It is something that happens when the conditions are right. And those conditions arise when we stop rejecting our internal landscape and begin listening to it. When we approach sensation with compassion rather than judgment. When we allow the body to lead rather than forcing it to follow the mind. When we honour the slow, organic intelligence of somatic unfolding. When we realize that each contraction is not a failure but an echo of a younger self seeking resolution.

This chapter closes with a simple but liberating recognition: **Letting go is not a path of effort — it is a path of intimacy.**

- The more intimately you inhabit your body, the more naturally it unwinds.
- The more gently you meet sensation, the more deeply release happens.
- The more fully you bring awareness to what arises, the more the past dissolves.

From here, the journey of awakening becomes less about striving and more about allowing. Less about transcending and more about descending — into the body, into sensation, into the truth that liberation is found not by escaping ourselves but by feeling ourselves completely.

As we move into the next chapter, we explore the deeper intelligence behind this entire process — the role of awareness itself as the healing agent that dissolves contraction and reorganizes the nervous system from the inside out.

Chapter

5

Awareness as the Healing Intelligence

Observer Mode and the Collapse of Identification

Observer mode is not a technique — it is a shift in consciousness. It is the moment awareness steps out of the stream of experience and recognizes itself as the space in which experience arises. This shift is subtle yet profound. When you enter observer mode, something loosens inside you. The tight grip of identification begins to dissolve, not through effort, but through clarity.

Most people live inside their experience — as the emotion, as the thought, as the contraction. The mind says, *I am angry. I am afraid. I am not enough.* The body tenses accordingly. The identity wraps itself around the sensation, merging with it completely. But observer mode interrupts this fusion. It introduces a new dimension into the moment: *This is something I am experiencing, not something I am.*

This simple differentiation collapses the illusion of identification. When awareness shifts from *inside* the emotion to *witnessing* the emotion, the emotional charge begins to soften. When awareness watches a thought rather than believing it, the thought loses its authority. When awareness notices a contraction without resisting it, the contraction begins to unwind.

Observer mode does not push anything away — its presence alone dissolves the glue that once held experience and identity together.

This is because identification requires unconsciousness. It requires forgetting that you are the awareness behind the experience. The moment awareness becomes aware of itself — aware that it is witnessing — identification can no longer sustain itself. The spell breaks. The structure of "me" begins to collapse not because it is attacked, but because its foundation is revealed as an assumption rather than a truth.

Observer mode is not dissociation. Dissociation disconnects you from experience. Observer mode connects you more deeply — to experience *and* to the spacious awareness that holds it. It is the most intimate form of presence. It does not create distance; it creates freedom.

In observer mode, you begin to feel the difference between sensation and self. The tightness in the chest is no longer "my anxiety" but simply tightness — sensation arising and dissolving in awareness. The heaviness in the heart is not "my sadness," but an energy moving through. Thoughts become events, not identity. Emotions become weather, not truth. The nervous system begins to reorganize itself around presence rather than reactivity.

This is the beginning of the collapse of identification. Identity is formed through the repeated merging of awareness with sensation, emotion, thought, and memory. Observer mode is the undoing of that merger. Every moment you witness without merging, without contracting, without believing the narrative, the identity loses density. The body softens. The mind quiets. The old "me" becomes more transparent, less convincing, less necessary.

Observer mode is the first taste of freedom because it reveals your true position:

- You are not inside your experience — your experience is inside you.
- You are not the thought — you are the one who notices the thought.
- You are not the contraction — you are the space in which it unfolds.

As this recognition deepens, a new way of being emerges — one in which awareness is no longer hijacked by survival patterns, and the nervous system begins to trust presence as its new baseline. This is the heart of somatic awakening: identity dissolving not through force, but through the quiet, steady power of awareness simply noticing itself.

The Difference Between Release, Catharsis, Opening, and Relaxation

As awareness deepens, the body begins to respond in ways that can feel unfamiliar. Sensation moves, emotion rises, energy flows, and boundaries soften. These experiences can appear similar on the surface, yet they arise from very different mechanisms within the nervous system. Understanding these distinctions helps you recognize what is unfolding within you — not so you can control it, but so you can meet each experience with clarity rather than confusion or expectation.

Somatic Release

Somatic release is the body unwinding a survival pattern. It is physiological, not emotional. It occurs when awareness meets contraction without pressure, creating enough safety for the nervous system to let go of something it once held for protection. Trembling, softening, breath opening, warmth, or spontaneous tears may arise — not as performance, but as completion. Somatic release resolves what the body could not complete in the moment of overwhelm.

Emotional Catharsis

Catharsis is emotional discharge — strong crying, yelling, shaking, or dramatic expression. While it can bring temporary relief, it does not necessarily reorganize the nervous system or dissolve identification. Catharsis ventilates the system; it does not always transform it. Without awareness, catharsis can reinforce old emotional loops rather than free you from them.

Energetic Opening

Energetic opening is a shift in the subtle field of the body — expansion, tingling, lightness, heat, or waves of bliss. These openings often follow moments of somatic softening, when the body becomes more permeable and less defended. They are signs of increased flow, but they do not inherently dissolve stored contraction unless awareness remains present.

Non-Dual Relaxation

Non-dual relaxation is not emotional or energetic — it is existential. It is the softening of the boundary between self and experience. Awareness rests as itself rather than as the content it witnesses. There is no effort, no strategy, no one trying to relax. The nervous system stops bracing against reality, and identity momentarily loosens into spaciousness.

These four experiences are not hierarchical — one is not better or "more spiritual" than another. They are simply different expressions of the system reorganizing itself in the presence of awareness. What matters is not which arises, but the quality of the witnessing that holds it.

Awareness does not seek to manipulate any of these states. It does not push for release, dramatize emotion, chase energetic highs, or cling to non-dual stillness. Its intelligence lies in meeting each moment exactly as it is. And as you continue through this chapter, you will see how this undemanding presence is precisely what allows the nervous system to reorganize from the inside out — softly, naturally, and in perfect alignment with its own timing.

Awareness as the Space That Dissolves Contraction

Contraction does not dissolve because we push against it. It dissolves because we bring it into the only environment where it no longer needs to protect us: awareness. Awareness is not an active force — it does not pry open the body, argue with tension, or manipulate sensation. Awareness is space. And space is the one condition in which holding becomes unnecessary.

When a contraction is met with resistance, it tightens. When it is ignored, it buries itself deeper. When it is analyzed, it becomes entangled in narrative. But when a contraction is met with spacious, nonjudgmental awareness — when it is simply allowed to be exactly as it is — it begins to soften on its own. Awareness creates room. It gives the body permission to release what it once had to hold.

Awareness dissolves contraction the way warmth melts ice: naturally, steadily, without force.

This happens because awareness removes the sense of threat. A contraction is a survival response — a physical expression of the body saying, *I need to hold this to stay safe.* But when awareness meets that contraction with softness and curiosity, the nervous system receives a new message: *You are safe now. You can relax.*

The contraction unwinds not because we commanded it to, but because it recognizes that the conditions for holding are no longer present. Awareness does nothing, yet everything happens within it.

In the presence of awareness, sensations begin to move. A tightness becomes a vibration. A heaviness becomes warmth. A frozen area begins to thaw. Space opens where there was previously density. The body is not being changed; it is remembering how to change itself. Awareness is simply the environment that allows the natural intelligence of the nervous system to reassert itself.

This is why awareness feels so healing. It does not fix the body — it reveals the body's capacity to restore itself. The more we rest in awareness, the more the body entrains to that openness. Over time, the system begins to trust that it no longer needs to brace. The protective layers that once defined our identity begin to melt. Old memories stored in tissue rise and complete. Emotional residue finds its way into motion and release. Presence becomes the default state rather than the exception.

This is the somatic essence of awakening: You do not dissolve contraction through effort. Contraction dissolves when the self who was resisting it steps aside.

Awareness is the stepping aside.

- It holds sensation without collapsing into it.
- It welcomes emotion without drowning in it.
- It sees thoughts without believing them.

In this environment, the nervous system reorganizes around truth instead of fear. The body no longer has to maintain old survival responses. The sense of self becomes less rigid, less defended, less tied to the patterns of contraction that once shaped it.

Awareness dissolves contraction not by changing the experience, but by changing our relationship to it. In the spaciousness of awareness, the body finally remembers its natural state — open, fluid, and unbound. And as contraction releases, what remains is clarity, presence, and the effortless sense of freedom that arises when nothing inside you is holding on.

The Shift from "I Am This Emotion" to "This Arises in Me"

One of the most transformative moments on the path of awakening is the shift from *identifying* with an emotion to *witnessing* it. At first, emotions feel personal. They feel like "me." The anger is *my* anger. The sadness is *my* sadness. The shame is *who I am.* The body contracts, the mind narrates, and awareness collapses into the experience so completely that there seems to be no separation between the emotion and the self.

But as awareness deepens, something subtle and extraordinary happens. The centre of perception shifts. Instead of being inside the emotion, you begin to notice the emotion. Instead of the thought “I am sad,” there is the recognition: *Sadness is arising in me.* A spaciousness opens. The tight fusion between identity and experience dissolves. The emotion remains, but the identification collapses.

This shift is not cognitive — it is somatic. The nervous system begins to relax enough for awareness to remain present while emotion arises. The body does not brace in the same way. The mind does not rush to interpret or defend. Awareness stays open, and in that openness, emotion is revealed not as identity but as energy, movement, sensation. It becomes an event, not a definition.

When awareness makes this shift, emotions no longer feel like threats. They are no longer overwhelming forces that must be controlled or suppressed. They are simply waves passing through the field of consciousness. And waves are not dangerous — they are natural. They rise, crest, and fall on their own. Nothing needs to be done except to remain present.

- “I am this emotion” is the language of survival.
- “This arises in me” is the language of awakening.

The former fuses the self with the emotion, making it heavy, sticky, and persistent. The latter restores freedom. In this recognition, the emotion loses its power to define or distort identity. It becomes part of the moment — not part of the self.

This shift reorganizes the entire internal landscape:

- Fear becomes a sensation, not a prophecy.
- Shame becomes a contraction, not a verdict.

- Grief becomes a movement, not a loss of worth.
- Anger becomes energy, not a flaw.

When emotions can arise without becoming “me,” the nervous system no longer needs to brace against them. The contraction that once held the emotion in place begins to unwind. The emotion moves because it no longer meets resistance. It completes because awareness is available to it. This is how awareness heals. It doesn’t erase emotions; it liberates them from the burden of being mistaken for identity.

In this state, you begin to feel yourself as the one who perceives, rather than the one who is consumed. You become the open space in which emotion occurs. And as this becomes more natural, the sense of self shifts irrevocably. You no longer live as a collection of reactions and stories. You live as the awareness that holds them.

Awakening is not the absence of emotion — it is the end of identification with it. When emotions arise in you rather than as you, the body relaxes, the mind clears, and the heart opens. You remain free, even as life moves through you.

How Witnessing Reorganizes the Nervous System

Witnessing is not passive. It is one of the most powerful forces in human transformation. When awareness witnesses experience — sensations, emotions, thoughts — it sends a message to the nervous system that fundamentally changes how the body organizes itself. It tells the system: *There is no danger here. You no longer need to protect yourself from this.* In that single recognition, physiology begins to shift.

The nervous system is always asking one question: *Am I safe?* When experience is met unconsciously, the body answers this question through old patterns — bracing, tightening, numbing, or collapsing. But when experience is witnessed — seen clearly, felt directly, held in awareness without resistance — the body receives a different answer. It senses presence where there was once overwhelm. It feels spaciousness where there was once entanglement. It detects that the moment is tolerable, even when intensity is present.

This is where reorganization begins. Witnessing interrupts the survival loop. The nervous system can no longer run on autopilot because awareness has stepped into the room. The reflex to fight, flee, freeze, or fawn softens. The body begins to shift out of sympathetic activation or dorsal collapse and into regulation. Breath returns. Sensation becomes fluid. The body starts updating its old conclusions: *This sensation is safe. This emotion can move. This experience can be felt without harm.*

Whatever the body was bracing against loses its power when it is seen. This is why witnessing feels like medicine. Awareness provides what was missing at the moment the contraction first formed: connection. The nervous system does not need the experience to disappear — it needs to know it isn't alone with it. When awareness stays present, the system realizes it is no longer in the past. It stops treating the present moment as if it is the original threat.

And as this recognition deepens, the nervous system reorganizes in real time. Tension begins to unwind because the body is no longer preparing for impact. Emotion rises and completes because nothing inside is suppressing it. Breath expands because vigilance is no longer constricting it. Energy moves because freeze is thawing.

The body recalibrates itself toward openness. Over time, witnessing creates a new baseline. The nervous system learns that awareness — not contraction — is the default state. The system becomes less reactive, not because life becomes easier, but because the internal environment becomes safer. The body trusts awareness in a way it once trusted contraction. And this trust is what allows awakening to stabilize.

As witnessing becomes habitual, the system begins to reorganize *before* contraction takes hold. An emotion rises, and the body meets it with space. A trigger appears, and the mind observes the activation rather than fusing with it. Sensation intensifies, and awareness stays steady. This is the nervous system reorganizing around presence instead of protection.

Witnessing is the mechanism by which the body learns freedom. It teaches the nervous system that experience can be felt without collapsing into it. It rewires the system to expect openness rather than threat. It transforms old patterns not by force, but by clarity. In the end, witnessing does what no technique, belief, or strategy can do: It returns the body to its natural state of coherence.

Through witnessing, the nervous system no longer organizes around survival — it organizes around awareness. And in that shift, awakening moves from concept to lived reality.

Stillness, Presence, and Somatic Coherence

Stillness is not the absence of movement — it is the absence of resistance. It is the state in which nothing inside you is pushing, pulling, bracing, or negotiating with the moment. Presence is the felt quality of that stillness becoming conscious. And somatic coherence is what emerges when the entire body aligns with that presence — when the nervous system, breath, heart, and awareness come into harmony.

Stillness is not something you create through effort. It is what remains when effort falls away. When awareness is no longer entangled in thought, when the body is no longer tightening against sensation, when emotions are no longer being resisted, a natural quietness reveals itself. This quietness is not passive; it is deeply alive. It is the fertile ground of healing, integration, and awakening.

Presence is how stillness expresses itself through awareness. It is the recognition of this moment as it is — unfiltered, undivided, unobscured by past or future.

Presence does not exclude sensation; it welcomes it. It does not silence emotion; it listens. It does not suppress the body; it includes it completely.

In presence, the body no longer senses danger in being felt. The nervous system relaxes its vigilance. Breath begins to settle naturally. The heart field stabilizes. The internal fragmentation created by years of survival patterns begins to reorganize. This is somatic coherence — the state in which the whole system operates from openness rather than protection.

Somatic coherence is what the body feels like when it stops bracing against life. It is the sensation of your chest not tightening before emotion rises.

- The belly softening rather than clenching.
- The throat opening instead of closing.
- The breath traveling freely from pelvis to heart.

- The mind quiet without effort, simply because there is nothing left to defend.

Coherence is not a peak state; it is a natural one. It is the baseline the body returns to when awareness is present and the nervous system feels safe. In this state, the body is no longer scattered across old memories or future anticipations. All of its intelligence moves in a unified direction — toward connection, openness, and truth.

Stillness is the absence of internal conflict. Presence is the awareness that perceives this harmony. Coherence is the body living in alignment with it.

When these three meet, the distinction between mind, body, and awareness dissolves. You experience yourself not as fragmented parts but as a single, unified field. This is why presence feels like home — because nothing inside you is at war with anything else.

In somatic coherence, awareness is no longer something you "practice." It becomes the nervous system's default orientation. The body knows how to stay open. The heart knows how to stay soft. The breath knows how to stay steady. The system reorganizes around truth rather than around survival.

This state is not the end of the path — it is the beginning of living it. Stillness gives rise to clarity. Presence gives rise to compassion. Coherence gives rise to freedom.

Together, they form the foundation upon which the rest of awakening unfolds — not as an escape from the body, but as the body's deepest remembering of what it always knew: *When nothing is held, everything becomes whole.*

Where Awareness Touches, Healing Begins

Awareness is not something we add to our experience — it is what remains when we stop resisting it. Throughout this chapter, we explored how awareness functions not as an idea, but as a living, healing intelligence that dissolves contraction, reorganizes the nervous system, and reveals a deeper truth beneath the patterns of survival. Awareness is not distant or abstract; it is the most intimate presence you can bring to yourself.

Observer mode showed us how identification collapses when awareness steps out of the story and into spacious witnessing. Awareness as space revealed that contraction softens not through effort but through permission.

The shift from "I am this emotion" to "This arises in me" demonstrated how identity loosens when emotion is no longer mistaken for self. Witnessing illuminated the nervous system's innate capacity to reorganize around presence instead of protection. Stillness, presence, and coherence revealed the body's natural state when it is no longer overwhelmed.

Together, these perspectives reveal a profound truth: Awareness is the medicine the body has been waiting for. Awareness does not heal by doing — it heals by being. It does not push anything away — it welcomes. It does not force release — it reveals the conditions under which release happens naturally.

Awareness reorganizes the entire system because it introduces what was missing when contraction formed: safety, connection, and spaciousness. When awareness is present, the body no longer feels alone with what it carries. It no longer has to brace or suppress. It can feel, express, unwind, and return to its natural coherence. Healing becomes not an achievement but an unfolding.

This chapter concludes with a simple recognition that changes everything: **Awareness is not just the witness of healing — it is the catalyst.**

As we move forward, we begin to see how this awareness, once stabilized, becomes the bridge between the human and the divine. In the next chapter, we explore what happens when the body is held not only by awareness but by something greater — something that dissolves fear, softens the ego, and ushers the system into a deeper state of safety and surrender.

Chapter

6

Somatic Surrender Into the Larger Presence

Why the Body Cannot Self-Regulate in Isolation

The body is not designed to regulate itself alone. Regulation is not a solitary achievement — it is a relational phenomenon woven into the fabric of human evolution. From the moment we enter the world, our nervous system learns safety through connection: the warmth of a caregiver's chest, the rhythm of another's breath, the soft gaze that tells us we belong. Before we develop language or thought, co-regulation is our first teacher. It is how the body learns, *I am safe enough to feel. I am safe enough to soften. I am safe enough to exist.*

This truth never stops being true. Even as adults, the nervous system does not fully self-regulate in isolation. It can downshift, settle, and unwind to some degree, but its deepest levels of safety — the kind that melt contraction, open the heart, quiet the ego, and dissolve survival patterns — are rarely reached alone. This is not weakness. It is biology.

Isolation places the nervous system in a subtle but persistent state of vigilance. When we are alone, some part of the system remains on alert, scanning the environment and the internal landscape for threat. This vigilance may be quiet, but it prevents the deepest layers of release. The body will not fully soften if it believes, even unconsciously, that it must guard itself.

Regulation happens most naturally in resonance — with another regulated nervous system, with the presence of safety, with a field that holds us. Human beings are wired to regulate through connection, not through independence. This is why healing often accelerates in the presence of someone grounded, attuned, and open. Their nervous system becomes a template, a signal, a reminder: *You can rest now.*

But co-regulation is not limited to other people. The body can also regulate in the presence of something greater — a force, a field, an intelligence beyond our individual self. Call it Source, consciousness, God, love, the divine, presence, or the greater field of awareness that underlies existence. Whatever name we give it, the effect is the same: the body feels held, and in that holding, its defences soften.

The nervous system responds to connection with something larger than the personal self in the same way it responds to a safe caregiver: it relaxes its vigilance, unwinds its contraction, and begins to reorganize. The ego, which formed to protect us in moments of aloneness, begins to loosen when it senses it is no longer alone. This recognition — the felt sense of being held — creates the conditions the body has been waiting for.

This is why meditation deepens when presence is palpable, why prayer calms the heart, why people feel profound peace in nature, and why spiritual awakening often involves moments of communion with something beyond the individual identity. The body recognizes resonance. It feels the larger field and regulates accordingly. Isolation fractures the system. Connection completes it.

Self-regulation becomes possible only when co-regulation has first established safety. The body learns openness in the presence of something that can hold it. It learns trust when it senses it is supported. It learns surrender when it feels it is not alone in the experience.

The body does not fail when it struggles to regulate in isolation — it is simply being faithful to its design. To soften, it needs resonance. To unwind, it needs holding. To transform, it needs connection.

In this way, divine co-regulation is not mystical — it is somatic. It is the nervous system responding to the greatest truth: You are not separate. You are not alone. You are held by something infinitely larger than your history, your fears, and the body's old survival patterns.

When the body feels this, regulation becomes effortless, and awakening stops being a solitary pursuit and becomes a relational unfolding with the very fabric of existence.

How Connection to Source Dissolves Fear

Fear does not dissolve through logic. It dissolves through contact with something larger than the self that fears. Fear is a contraction — an instinctive narrowing of the nervous system in response to perceived threat. But fear only survives in a state of perceived aloneness. It needs separation to exist. The moment the nervous system senses true connection — especially connection to Source, to the greater field of awareness that holds all experience — the very foundation of fear begins to unravel.

Connection to Source is not a belief. It is a felt experience.

- a softening in the chest
- a widening behind the eyes
- a deepening of breath
- a subtle but undeniable sense of being supported, accompanied, and surrounded by an intelligence far greater than the individual identity

When this connection is felt, the nervous system enters resonance with a state that is deeper, wiser, and infinitely more stable than the survival patterns it's used to running. Fear cannot maintain itself in the presence of this resonance — not because fear is pushed away, but because the body realizes it no longer needs to guard.

Fear dissolves not through force, but through being held. Source is the ultimate co-regulator. It requires no words, no effort, no technique. Its presence alone communicates safety.

- When the body feels that it is held by something vast, fear loses its urgency
- When the heart senses it is not alone, fear loses its authority.
- When awareness remembers its unity with Source, fear loses its meaning.

Fear is a signal of disconnection — disconnection from the body, disconnect from presence, disconnect from the larger field of intelligence that animates existence. But the moment connection to Source is restored, the nervous system receives an unmistakable message: *You can rest. You are supported. You can open. You can release.*

Fear collapses because the nervous system no longer perceives itself as the sole container of experience. In connection with Source:

- The ego no longer feels responsible for controlling everything.
- The body no longer believes it must tighten to survive.
- The mind no longer assumes that it must anticipate every threat.
- The heart no longer feels like it must protect itself from the unknown.

The system reorganizes around a deeper intelligence — one that does not contract in the face of life, but flows with it. Fear becomes unnecessary when the body senses that something larger is holding it, guiding it, and moving through it.

This is why many spiritual traditions describe profound peace in moments of surrender to the divine. It is not psychological — it is physiological. The nervous system recognizes safety in the presence of Source. It entrains to the frequency of love, spaciousness, and coherence. It relaxes into what is real.

Connection to Source dissolves fear because fear cannot coexist with oneness. Fear requires separation to survive. When you feel Source — when you feel the vastness that holds you — separation collapses. And with it, the fear that was built on the illusion of being alone collapses too.

In the presence of Source, the body remembers its true nature: Open. Safe. Guided. Held by something infinitely greater than anything it once feared.

Spiritual Presence as Somatic Safety

Spiritual presence is not an idea the mind holds — it is a state the body feels. It is the quiet, unmistakable sense that something larger, wiser, and infinitely benevolent is here. Not conceptually, but tangibly. When true presence is felt, the nervous system receives a kind of reassurance it cannot generate on its own: *You are safe. You are supported. You are not carrying this moment alone.*

This is why spiritual presence becomes somatic safety. The body listens not to thoughts, but to signals. Not to philosophy, but to resonance. Not to belief, but to felt experience.

When presence fills the space around and within you, the body relaxes. Something inside stops gripping. The survival patterns loosen their hold. The heart softens, the breath deepens, and your awareness becomes less fragmented. The body recognizes that it is in the company of something that asks for nothing, demands nothing, and imposes nothing — only offers support.

Spiritual presence communicates safety without a single word.

- it quiets fear without opposing it
- it dissolves contraction without effort
- it regulates the nervous system without technique

This is because spiritual presence is coherence — the purest form of it. It is the field of unity, spaciousness, and unconditional acceptance. When the body encounters this field, it begins to entrain to it. Just as one tuning fork vibrates when placed near another, your nervous system begins to match the frequency of presence.

This is why people often feel calmer, clearer, and more open in the presence of awakened beings, in sacred spaces, in nature, or in moments of deep meditation. The body senses the absence of threat and the abundance of support. It reorganizes itself accordingly.

Spiritual presence is somatic safety because it offers what the body craves most:

- a field with no judgment
- space with no expectation
- openness with no pressure
- love with no conditions
- a holding that asks nothing in return

In this environment, the body's defences become unnecessary. The vigilance that once defined your inner world begins to fade. The nervous system drops out of the survival loop and into its natural state of regulation. This shift does not come from believing in presence — it comes from feeling it.

When spiritual presence fills your awareness, the body begins to trust what it senses. Trust is what the nervous system needs in order to release. Without trust, contraction persists. With trust, opening becomes effortless.

Spiritual presence creates the internal conditions the body requires to heal — conditions it cannot create in isolation. It gives the nervous system a reference point for safety that is deeper than any strategy, deeper than any technique, deeper than the ego's limited attempts to self-soothe. Presence does what the mind cannot: it changes the body's perception of reality at the deepest level.

When presence is here, the body knows.

- it knows it is held
- it knows it can rest
- it knows the moment does not have to be survived — it can be experienced

This is the somatic foundation of spiritual awakening: the felt sense that something greater is with you, in you, and holding you. And in that holding, your entire system returns to the truth it had forgotten: *You were never meant to navigate life alone.*

Co-Regulation as the Bridge from Ego to Awareness

The ego forms in moments of aloneness, but awareness deepens in moments of connection. Between these two states — separation and unity — there is a bridge, and that bridge is co-regulation. Co-regulation is not merely emotional support or relational comfort; it is the nervous system's way of remembering what the ego forgot: *You are not meant to carry this experience alone.*

The ego is a solitary structure. It developed in isolation. It learned to protect in isolation. It learned to control, anticipate, defend, and contract — all in isolation.

Because of this, the ego cannot unravel through isolation. It needs a counter-experience: a nervous system outside itself that signals safety, resonance, and presence. Co-regulation provides that missing piece. It gives the body a felt sense of support that the ego cannot generate internally. Co-regulation does for the nervous system what the ego could never do: It relaxes it.

When you are in the presence of someone grounded, open, attuned, or embodied — whether a teacher, a partner, a friend, or even a stranger — their regulation invites your system into a deeper truth. They are not fixing you; they are anchoring a frequency your nervous system recognizes as safe. The body relaxes not because of who they are, but because of what their presence communicates: *You can let go now. You can open. You are not alone.* And as the body softens, the ego softens. As the ego softens, awareness expands. This is the bridge.

In co-regulation, the nervous system experiences what the ego fears most: letting go of control. And yet, paradoxically, this is exactly what it needs. When you feel someone else holding presence with you — truly seeing, attuning, and allowing — you don't collapse; you open. You don't disappear; you emerge. You don't lose yourself; you return to yourself.

Co-regulation becomes a living demonstration that safety and openness are not opposites. They are partners. They are prerequisites for awakening.

Over time, the body internalizes this experience. The nervous system learns what safety feels like, not as a concept but as a somatic truth. And once learned, it becomes reproducible internally. This is how co-regulation evolves into self-regulation — not through isolation, but through the memory of connection. This is also how co-regulation becomes a bridge into deeper awareness.

When the body is regulated, awareness is no longer hijacked by survival patterns. Presence becomes accessible. The mind quiets. The emotional field softens. Identification loosens. In this openness, awareness can finally witness experience without fusing with it. The ego loses its urgency because the body is no longer in a defensive state.

Co-regulation, then, is not just a relational gift — it is a spiritual one.

- It brings the nervous system out of separation and into resonance.
- It brings the heart out of protection and into connection.
- It brings the mind out of survival and into awareness.

Through co-regulation, the ego's grip loosens, and the body begins to trust the very state that ego once feared: spacious awareness. This is the moment awakening becomes possible — not because the ego is defeated, but because it is no longer needed.

Co-regulation is the bridge from the self that survives to the self that remembers. It is the path from contraction back into consciousness. It is how the body is escorted out of fear and into the field of awareness that has always held it.

Trust, Surrender, and the Descent Out of Survival

Trust and surrender are not mental decisions — they are somatic shifts. They happen not when we tell ourselves to let go, but when the body finally realizes it no longer needs to protect itself. Trust is the nervous system relaxing its vigilance. Surrender is the ego releasing its grip. And both are only possible when the system senses it is being held by something greater — by presence, by connection, by Source.

Survival is an upward, effortful movement. It lifts the energy out of the body and into the mind. It tightens the shoulders, braces the chest, contracts the belly, and places the nervous system on high alert. In survival, nothing can be trusted, because the system is organized around the assumption: *I am alone. I must manage everything myself.* Trust begins the moment this assumption is challenged by direct experience.

When something larger enters the field — something steady, attuned, coherent, and unconditionally present — the survival system pauses. It hesitates. It listens. It scans for threat...and finds none. This is the first crack in the armour. A softening that seems almost accidental: a longer exhale, a subtle release in the heart, a loosening in the throat. These are not psychological events — they are the body's first steps out of survival.

True trust arises when the body feels supported, not when the mind is convinced.

Surrender is simply the next breath after trust.

- It is what happens naturally when the body realizes it no longer needs to brace.
- It is the exhale that was held for years.
- It is the melting of tension that had become invisible.
- It is the softening of the ego's insistence that it must stay in charge.

Surrender is not collapse. It is not passivity. It is not giving up. Surrender is the nervous system's recognition that openness is now safer than contraction. It is the body remembering what the ego forgot: *I am held. I am guided. I am safe.*

This descent out of survival is not dramatic — it is gentle. Slow. Organic. It unfolds in waves. Heavy emotions rise but feel less overwhelming. Old contractions surface but no longer dictate behaviour. The mind still tries to anticipate, but awareness stays steady enough that anticipation loses its power.

As surrender deepens, the body moves downward — not into darkness, but into depth. Into the belly, into the heart, into the ground, into the present moment. Energy that once lived in the upper chest and mind begins to settle. You become heavier, but in the way a tree is heavy: rooted, supported by the earth rather than suspended in effort.

This descent is the opposite of transcendence. It is embodiment. It is Presence becoming physical. It is consciousness descending into the tissues, the breath, the nervous system.

When trust and surrender become embodied, the survival system rewrites its rules. It no longer expects danger. It no longer prepares for impact. It no longer sees the world through the lens of fear.

Instead, it begins to operate from coherence — responding, not reacting; opening, not bracing; experiencing, not defending. This is the somatic foundation of awakening:

- The moment the body realizes it is safe enough to release the protective patterns that once formed your identity.
- The moment the nervous system descends out of survival and into presence.
- The moment you feel, perhaps for the first time, that you are not carrying life — life is carrying you.

Trust opens the door. Surrender walks through it. And in this descent, you return to the deepest truth of your being: You were never meant to navigate your humanity alone.

The Body Awakens When It Feels Held

The journey through this chapter brings us to a profound realization: awakening is not something we accomplish alone. It is something that emerges when the body feels supported by a presence greater than the self that has spent years, or even decades, trying to survive by itself. Co-regulation — whether through another human, through nature, or through the direct felt sense of Source — is not a spiritual luxury. It is the biological foundation that allows awakening to take root.

The body does not relax because we tell it to. It relaxes because something in the field tells it: *You are safe. You are seen. You are not alone.*

This chapter revealed why the nervous system cannot self-regulate in isolation, how connection to Source dissolves fear, and why spiritual presence generates somatic safety in a way no mental strategy can. We explored how co-regulation becomes the bridge from ego to awareness — how the very patterns that formed in aloneness begin to soften only when the system encounters resonance, steadiness, and unconditional support. And we saw how trust and surrender are not abstract virtues but embodied states that arise naturally when the body senses that survival is no longer required.

Together, these teachings illuminate a simple truth: We awaken not by escaping our humanity, but by letting something larger hold it.

The ego dissolves when it is no longer forced to protect. Fear dissolves when the body feels accompanied. Contraction dissolves when presence enters the room. Identity dissolves when awareness meets support.

The divine is not separate from the body — it is what the body has been longing to feel. It is the resonance that reorganizes the nervous system. It is the presence that melts the bracing. It is the safety that makes awakening possible.

This chapter closes with a reminder that is both tender and powerful: You do not have to awaken alone. You were never meant to.

As you move forward, the path ahead becomes less about effort and more about allowing yourself to be held — by Source, by presence, by life itself. In the next chapter, you will see how the body's illusions of separation begin to unravel when the protective patterns of the ego soften, revealing the truth that has always been beneath them.

III

Releasing the Ego Through the Body

Chapter

7

The Somatic Illusion of Separation

How Contraction Creates "Self"

The sense of "self" that most people live with is not a spiritual truth — it is a somatic contraction. What we call "me" is, in its earliest and most fundamental form, the body tightening around experience. Before the mind builds narrative, before identity takes shape, the nervous system creates a boundary: a subtle, protective narrowing in response to overwhelm. That narrowing becomes the first outline of the separate self.

Contraction is the body's attempt to contain what feels unmanageable. When sensation becomes too intense, when emotion arrives faster than we can process, when connection feels unpredictable, the nervous system instinctively tightens. In that moment, awareness collapses inward. The body forms an inner perimeter, and this perimeter is interpreted by the mind as "I." It is not that contraction follows identity — it *forms* it.

The self, as most people know it, is the story the mind tells about the areas of the body that have not yet been able to relax.

Every tightening in the chest, every clench in the jaw, every holding in the belly contributes to the illusion of a discrete "me." These somatic patterns shape perception. They create blind spots. They define what we fear, what we avoid, what we pursue, and what we believe is possible. The mind then weaves these patterns into narrative: *This is just who I am. This is how I am. This is the way I've always been.* But behind each of these stories is a contraction the body once created in order to cope.

Contraction makes the world feel external and separate. When the body tightens, it feels as though life is "out there" and we are "in here" — a fragment isolated from the whole. This is the origin of duality. Not philosophy. Not thought. Contraction. A tightening that creates the illusion of two: the experiencer and the experienced.

And because contraction reduces our capacity, it also creates a distorted sense of self. A small self. A defended self. A self organized around what it must avoid rather than what it truly is. When we live inside contraction long enough, we mistake the boundaries of our bracing for the boundaries of our identity.

This is why awakening cannot be achieved through thought alone. The mind can see unity, but the body continues living inside the contours of contraction. The sense of "me" persists because the body is still holding itself in a shape formed by past overwhelm. Until the contraction softens, identity remains.

Yet the moment contraction loosens, even slightly, the sense of self begins to shift. Openness replaces boundary. Flow replaces tightness. Awareness expands past the perimeter of the body. The "I" that once felt solid becomes fluid, spacious, permeable. What we believed was identity reveals itself to be nothing more than a set of survival patterns the body had once adopted.

This is the somatic illusion of separation: Contraction creates "self," but when contraction dissolves, so does the illusion.

The true self is not found in the tightening — it is found in what appears when the tightening is gone.

The Body as the First Place Ego Forms

The ego does not begin as a thought, belief, or psychological structure. Long before the mind develops language to describe itself, the body has already shaped the first version of "me." The ego begins somatically. It begins as a tightening, a withdrawal, a subtle bracing against experience that becomes the earliest boundary between self and world.

In infancy, the nervous system has no narrative. It has no identity. It has no sense of "I." What it does have is sensation — raw, unfiltered sensation — and a rapidly forming survival system that learns, moment by moment, how to cope with a world far too overwhelming to meet all at once. When the sensation becomes too intense, the body contracts. When emotional charge becomes too much to process, the body suppresses. When connection feels unstable, the body pulls inward. These early physiological responses become the somatic template of the ego.

The body becomes the container that the ego later fills with story. This is why the ego feels so personal: it is built into the tissue. It lives in the breath patterns we learned as children. It lives in the way our shoulders rise in anticipation of conflict. It lives in the habitual clenching of the belly, the collapse of the heart, the rigid holding in the jaw. The mind eventually claims these patterns as identity, but the body created them long before the mind had any say.

The ego forms as the body's attempt to create coherence where there was once overwhelm. It forms as a boundary, not out of preference, but out of protection. It forms as a contraction, not out of choice, but out of necessity.

When a child feels unsafe, unseen, or emotionally unsupported, the nervous system responds in the only way it knows how: by creating an internal perimeter of safety through tension and withdrawal. That perimeter is the proto-ego. It is the somatic starting point of "I exist here, and the world exists there." Before the mind names this separation, the body has already enacted it.

This is why the ego cannot be dissolved through thought. Thought did not create it. The nervous system did. The mind's interpretation of ego — its stories, fears, personas, and beliefs — are secondary. They are the narrative architecture built on top of the body's foundational pattern of holding. To work only with the mental ego is to work with the shadow of the problem, not its root. The root is somatic: the body holding itself in a shape of separation.

And because the body created the first version of ego, it is also the place where ego must dissolve. It dissolves not through insight, but through release. Not through understanding, but through presence. Not through transcendence, but through intimacy with the sensations that formed the original boundaries.

When the body softens and its contractions unwind, the ego loses its foundation. The mind's stories fall away because the somatic tension they were built upon is no longer there. The sense of a separate "me" weakens because the body is no longer holding itself apart. What once felt like a fixed identity becomes fluid, spacious, and permeable.

The body was the first place ego formed. It is also the first place ego unravels. Awakening begins not by transcending the body, but by entering it — by meeting the very contractions that once created the illusion of separation and allowing them to finally, mercifully, release.

Shame, Fear, and Unworthiness as Stored Identity

Shame, fear, and unworthiness do not begin as beliefs. They begin as sensations — intense, overwhelming sensations the young nervous system had no capacity to process. Before they become stories in the mind, they become contractions in the body. And when these contractions repeat often enough, they solidify into identity.

Shame is not originally the thought *"There is something wrong with me."* It is the burn in the chest, the collapse in the heart, the sinking in the belly. It is the body folding inward to become smaller, safer, less visible. The mind interprets this posture later, translating the contraction into narrative. But the body felt it first.

Fear is not the belief *"I am in danger."* It is the tightening behind the ribs, the freezing in the diaphragm, the rapid drawing upward of energy. It is the nervous system preparing for impact long before the mind can describe why. Fear becomes identity because the contraction becomes familiar — an internal state repeated so often that the body assumes it is who we are.

Unworthiness is not the conclusion *"I don't deserve good."* It is the heaviness in the gut, the constricted throat when receiving kindness, the subtle shrinking away from love. Before the mind forms the story of undeserving, the body has already created the shape of withdrawal.

These states become identity because the nervous system organizes itself around them. The body learns:

- *stay small to stay safe*
- *stay alert to stay safe*
- *stay hidden to stay safe*
- *stay separate to stay safe*

And the mind, attempting to make sense of the body's ongoing contraction, builds meaning around it. Shame becomes "me." Fear becomes "my nature." Unworthiness becomes "who I am." But none of these are identity — they are stored survival states.

They are the body's memory of past overwhelm, encoded through muscle tension, breath patterns, and emotional suppression. And because they are stored in the body, they do not dissolve when beliefs change. You can believe you are worthy while your chest is still collapsed. You can know you are safe while your belly is still clenched. You can understand you are lovable while your heart is still braced.

This is why emotional work often feels incomplete without somatic work. The mind may rewrite the story, but the body is still living the old one.

Shame, fear, and unworthiness dissolve not through reframing but through feeling. Through presence meeting the contraction. Through awareness entering the exact place the nervous system once shut down. Through allowing the body to complete what was never completed: the emotion, the expression, the movement, the breath.

As these contractions unwind, the identity built upon them unravels. Shame releases, and the heart lifts. Fear softens, and the breath deepens. Unworthiness melts, and the body expands into the fullness of its natural state.

What remains is not a new identity, but the absence of the old one. A spaciousness. A clarity. A grounded openness that does not need to define itself because it is no longer bracing against experience.

The illusion of separation begins to crumble the moment we see that what we called "self" was simply stored emotion — sensation waiting to be met, tension waiting to be honoured, humanity waiting to be felt.

In releasing these somatic imprints, the body remembers its original nature: not shameful, not fearful, not unworthy — but open, whole, and inherently connected.

The Collapse of the False Self Through Release

The false self is not dismantled through insight — it is dissolved through release. It is not a psychological structure that must be defeated, nor a spiritual flaw that must be transcended. It is a somatic configuration: a complex weave of contractions, suppressed emotion, bracing patterns, and protective responses that once kept you safe. The false self collapses not when the mind understands its illusion, but when the body no longer holds the tension that gave it shape.

Every piece of the false self is anchored in the body. The perfectionist is anchored in the tight jaw and lifted chest. The pleaser is anchored in the collapsed heart and shallow breath. The achiever is anchored in the contracted diaphragm and forward-leaning posture. The protector is anchored in the clenched belly and vigilant eyes.

Identity forms around these survival shapes. The mind interprets the body's posture and declares, *This is who I am.* But identity is simply the story wrapped around unresolved somatic experience. The moment those underlying contractions release, the story begins to unravel.

Release is the moment the body stops defending against what it once believed it had to brace for. It is the moment sensation moves freely instead of getting trapped. It is the moment the breath returns to spaces inside you that had been closed for years. It is the moment the nervous system realizes the threat is no longer present. And when this happens, something profound occurs: the somatic foundation of the false self dissolves.

As the body unwinds, the sense of "me" shifts. A contraction softens — and the identity built upon it no longer feels solid. A long-held emotion completes — and the narrative that justified it loses its weight. A bracing pattern melts — and the personality trait that defended it becomes irrelevant.

You are not actively letting go of the false self. The false self is dissolving because there is nothing left in the body to hold it in place.

This collapse is not dramatic. It is quiet. Organic. Barely noticeable until suddenly it is unmistakable. You look for the familiar tension — and it is gone. You wait for the old reaction — and it does not come. You try to embody the old identity — and it feels foreign, as if you are stepping into clothes that no longer fit.

Release rearranges the internal landscape so completely that the old self cannot reassemble. The stories lose their charge. The fears lose their authority. The roles lose their gravitational pull. The world no longer feels like something you must brace against, and without that bracing, the "self" that lived in defence dissolves.

This is the collapse of the false self:

- not destruction, but dissolution
- not effort, but allowing
- not transcendence, but embodiment

What remains is not a new identity, but space. Space where contraction once lived. Space where fear once spoke. Space where shame once crouched.

In that space, a deeper truth reveals itself — not as an idea, but as a lived experience. A self that is not built on contraction, but on openness. A self that is not shaped by fear, but by presence. A self that is not manufactured, but remembered.

The false self collapses through release, and in that collapse, the illusion of separation begins to unravel — revealing the spacious, undivided awareness that was always underneath.

The Beginning of Non-Dual Emergence

Non-duality does not begin as a mystical realization — it begins as a physiological shift. It begins the moment contraction loosens enough for awareness to expand beyond the boundaries of the body's old survival patterns. When the somatic imprint of "self" softens, even slightly, a space opens where separation once lived. In that space, something new — and ancient — emerges: the direct felt sense that you are not separate from what you experience. Non-dual emergence is not an insight the mind achieves. It is a state the body allows.

As the contractions that shaped identity begin to dissolve, the nervous system stops bracing against life. Sensation becomes less threatening. Emotion becomes more fluid. The protective walls that once defined the "me" begin to thin. And in the absence of those walls, awareness naturally expands. You begin to sense yourself not merely as a person having an experience, but as the field in which the experience unfolds.

The distinction between "in here" and "out there" grows softer. The distance between self and life closes. Presence begins to feel continuous rather than localized.

This is not yet full non-duality — but it is the beginning. It is the nervous system's first glimpse at what it feels like to exist without the constant somatic boundaries that once created the illusion of separation. It is the early stage of unity becoming embodied.

For many, this emergence is not dramatic. It is subtle. It often shows up as:

- A sudden ease in the breath where there was once tightness
- a moment of spaciousness behind the eyes
- a softening of the heart that seems uncaused
- a sense that emotion is arising "within" the field rather than "inside" a person
- a quiet recognition that awareness is bigger than the body

These small openings are profound because they reveal the truth the ego could never access within contraction: that who we are is not a tight centre inside the chest, but the open space in which the chest exists. Not the thoughts moving through the mind, but the awareness that holds them. Not the one struggling to awaken, but the consciousness in which the struggle appears and dissolves.

When the body stops organizing around fear, awareness becomes free to reveal itself. Non-dual emergence is the moment the nervous system stops resisting the present moment, and unity begins to be *felt*, not imagined. It is the shift from trying to understand oneness to sensing it directly. The shift from perceiving life through the ego's narrow lens to perceiving through the body's expanding openness.

As this emergence deepens, the experience of being a separate self begins to feel less convincing. Not because you reject it, but because it loses its somatic foundation. Without contraction to reinforce the illusion of "me," the identity constructed by the mind begins to dissolve naturally. What remains is presence. Spaciousness. Awareness experiencing itself without division.

This is the beginning of non-dual emergence: the nervous system relaxing enough for consciousness to remember its own nature, the body softening enough for awareness to flow without boundary, the self loosening enough for unity to reveal itself in the simplest, most ordinary moments.

It is the quiet beginning of a profound truth becoming embodied: separation was never real — only somatically rehearsed. And as the body unwinds, the truth of unity emerges on its own.

When the Body Releases, the Illusion Falls Away

Separation is not a philosophical mistake — it is a somatic one. It lives in the body as contraction, suppression, bracing, and emotional residue. What we have called "self" for most of our lives is simply the shape the nervous system adopted in response to overwhelm. The illusion of separation is sustained not by belief, but by tension; not by thought, but by physiology. And as the body unwinds, the illusion begins to dissolve.

In this chapter, we explored how contraction becomes identity, how the ego is born first in the body before it becomes a story in the mind, how shame, fear, and unworthiness are not traits but stored survival states, and how release is the quiet collapse of the false self. We saw how non-duality does not appear through effort but through the gradual softening of the patterns that once created the boundary between "self" and "life."

The truth revealed here is simple, profound, and deeply liberating: **When the body lets go, the self we thought we were lets go with it.**

As these somatic structures dissolve, what emerges is not a new identity, but an absence of division. Awareness expands. The heart opens. The boundary between inner and outer thins. Life begins to feel less like something happening to you and more like something happening through you. Unity stops being a concept and becomes a sensation — subtle, intimate, and unmistakably true.

The somatic illusion of separation falls away not because we reject the ego, but because we no longer inhabit the contractions that kept it alive. What remains is presence — wide, effortless, and whole. What remains is the truth of who we are when nothing inside us is bracing against life.

This chapter closes with a recognition that prepares the ground for everything that follows: **The path to awakening is not an ascent out of the body — it is a descent into it.** Into sensation. Into release. Into openness.

And through this descent, the illusion that we are separate dissolves, and the body becomes not a barrier to awakening, but its doorway.

Chapter

8

Trauma, Identity, and the False Self

How Unresolved Emotions Shape Personality

Personality is not who we are — it is who we became when we could not fully feel what was happening to us. Before it becomes a set of traits or behaviours, personality begins as a collection of incomplete emotional experiences stored in the body. These unresolved emotions — fear, shame, grief, anger, confusion, longing — become the scaffolding around which the "self" organizes. Not because they define our essence, but because the nervous system shapes identity around whatever it must manage, avoid, or suppress to survive.

When an emotion is too overwhelming for a child's system to process, the body contracts to contain it. That contraction becomes a pattern. That pattern becomes familiar. And familiarity becomes "me."

The child who could not express anger becomes the adult who identifies as calm, agreeable, or conflict-avoidant. The child who felt invisible becomes the adult who identifies as independent, self-reliant, or emotionally distant. The child who felt unsafe becomes the adult who identifies as vigilant, analytical, or controlling. The child who felt unworthy becomes the adult who identifies as helpful, overachieving, or self-sacrificing.

These identities are not expressions of our true nature — they are compensations for emotions we were once unable to feel.

Unresolved emotions shape personality because the body organizes itself around avoiding re-experiencing what once felt unbearable. If abandonment was overwhelming, the system shapes a personality that clings or one that never attaches. If shame was overwhelming, the system shapes a personality that overperforms or one that hides. If fear was overwhelming, the system shapes a personality that anticipates, protects, and controls every detail.

The mind later interprets these adaptations as traits, preferences, or flaws. But beneath every personality structure lies the same truth: the body is navigating unfinished emotional business.

This is why personality feels both familiar and confining. It is not our natural expression — it is our survival expression. It is the shape the nervous system took when it learned which emotions were too dangerous to feel fully. It is a pattern of bracing held long enough to look like identity.

These emotional imprints don't just shape how we behave — they shape how we perceive:

- A person with unprocessed fear sees the world as uncertain.
- A person with unprocessed shame sees themselves as insufficient.
- A person with unprocessed grief sees connection as risky.
- A person with unprocessed anger sees boundaries as dangerous.

The nervous system filters reality through the emotional charges it still holds, and the personality becomes the mask we wear to navigate life with these undigested imprints still inside us.

But these "personality traits" begin to dissolve the moment we feel the emotions underneath them. As trapped anger moves, the calm persona softens into authentic clarity. As shame unwinds, the overachiever relaxes into presence. As fear releases, the controller opens into trust. As grief moves, the avoider becomes capable of intimacy.

Personality loosens because the emotional contractions that sustained it loosen. This is the heart of somatic awakening: *You do not lose who you truly are — you lose who you had to become.* And in the absence of those unresolved emotions, the self that remains is not a strategy, not a defence, not a compensation — but a direct, unfiltered expression of your essence.

Personality shifts not because we try to change ourselves, but because the body finally releases what shaped us in the first place.

The "Small Self" as a Survival Structure

The "small self" is not a flaw in consciousness — it is a survival achievement. It is the version of you the nervous system assembled when life felt too overwhelming, too fast, too unpredictable for your young body to meet fully. Long before the mind formed its narratives of identity, the body crafted a structure — a condensed, defended, manageable version of self — to help you endure what you could not yet process. This "small self" is not who you are. It is who you became in order to stay safe.

The body's first priority is survival, not authenticity. When sensation, emotion, or relational intensity exceeded your capacity, the nervous system contracted around the moment. In that contraction, something narrowed — not just in your physiology, but in your sense of identity. The self became smaller, tighter, more contained. It became a structure of limits, because limits were safer than openness.

The small self is born from this contraction. It forms through:

- **A restricted breath** — because breathing fully made you too vulnerable.
- **A tightened chest** — because feeling fully was too overwhelming.
- **A frozen diaphragm** — because expressing emotion felt dangerous.
- **A collapsed heart** — because connection couldn't be trusted.
- **A rigid mind** — because predictability felt safer than presence.

These physiological patterns become the shape of the "me" that navigates the world. A self organized around avoidance, control, anticipation, pleasing, performing, or shrinking — whichever strategies helped you survive your early environment.

The small self is not a personality; it is a protective architecture. It keeps life at a distance so you don't feel too much at once. It narrows your emotional range so nothing overwhelms you. It limits your expression so you do not risk rejection. It contracts your presence so you do not draw attention to wounds that were never held.

This is why the small self feels fragile: it is built on the foundation of unprocessed experience. It is not strong; it is tense. It is not empowered; it is defended. It is not authentic; it is adaptive. To live as the small self is to live as a contraction, not as consciousness.

And yet, this survival structure deserves compassion, not condemnation. It formed to protect you when no one else could. It held you together when you had no internal capacity, no external support, and no way of understanding the emotional storms moving through your body. The small self is a testament to your resilience.

But awakening cannot stabilize inside this structure. The small self must eventually soften for awareness to expand. Not through force. Not through rejection. But through safety — through allowing the body to feel what it once could not feel, releasing what it once had to suppress, and unwinding the contraction that once defined your edges.

As the survival structure loosens, the small self begins to dissolve — not because you try to transcend it, but because it is no longer needed. The nervous system reorganizes around openness instead of defence. Presence expands. Consciousness breathes deeper into the body. And the self that emerges is no longer small.

This is the shift from survival to awakening: The body releases the structure it built to protect you, and what remains is the larger Self — the uncontracted, undefended, spacious expression of who you truly are.

Why the Ego Fights to Maintain Familiar Contraction

The ego does not fight because it is malicious — it fights because it is terrified. It clings to familiar contraction not out of stubbornness, but out of survival logic. To the ego, contraction *is* safety. Tightening is protection. Familiarity is security. Even if the pattern is painful, limiting, or exhausting, the ego prefers it over the unknown, because the unknown feels like danger to a nervous system shaped by unresolved experience.

The ego was built inside contraction. It was shaped by the body's earliest attempts to manage overwhelm. It formed around the breath that shortened, the belly that clenched, the heart that closed, the emotion that froze.

These contractions became the ego's home. And the ego fights to preserve the home it knows — even if that home was built in fear.

The ego interprets release as threat because release means change. Change means unpredictability. Unpredictability resembles the very conditions that caused the original contraction. So the ego concludes: *Stay how you are. Stay tense. Stay small. Stay familiar.* It would rather maintain a known suffering than risk an unknown openness.

Familiar contraction creates a sense of identity. The ego thinks:

- "This tightness is me."
- "This vigilance is me."
- "This shame is me."
- "This hyper-awareness is me."
- "These limits are who I am."

So when contraction starts to soften, the ego panics. Not because softening is harmful, but because it destabilizes the foundation of a self constructed through years of bracing. The ego confuses release with death — not physical death, but the death of the only identity it has ever known.

This is why the ego resists healing. Not because it wants to suffer, but because it equates release with annihilation. The body begins to open, and the ego fears losing control. Emotion begins to rise, and the ego fears being overwhelmed again. Breath deepens, and the ego fears what may surface in that spaciousness. Presence expands, and the ego fears dissolving into the very awareness that holds it.

To the ego, openness is not peace — it is vulnerability. It is exposure. It is returning to a state in which the original wound was felt. So it contracts. It argues. It distracts. It tries to pull you back into the familiar shape of the old self.

The ego fights for familiar contraction because contraction once saved you. It is a loyal protector, even when the threat has long passed. It holds the old state together because the nervous system has not yet learned a new one. It braces not against life, but against the possibility of encountering what was never processed.

But as the body begins to feel safe again — as awareness is brought to sensation, as co-regulation offers support, as presence becomes more stable — the ego's grip loosens. The familiar contraction no longer feels necessary. The nervous system begins to experience openness as safety rather than risk.

And in this shift, the ego stops fighting. Not because it has been conquered, but because it has been reassured.

The ego releases its hold when the body feels safe enough to release what it once protected. It softens when it realizes it no longer needs to contract around past overwhelm. It dissolves when the nervous system reorganizes around presence instead of fear.

In the end, the ego does not have to be defeated — it has to be liberated. Freed from the contractions that taught it who it believed it had to be. Freed from the burden of guarding a self built from past pain. Freed enough to let the larger Self emerge from beneath the small one.

When the body stops clinging to contraction, the ego finally stops fighting. And in that moment, authenticity begins.

Somatic Innocence: The Ego Was Always Protection

The ego is often portrayed as an obstacle, a distortion, or a spiritual problem to be overcome. But when we look through the lens of the body, the ego reveals itself as something profoundly innocent. It was never the enemy — it was the protector. It formed not out of malice or selfishness, but out of necessity. It emerged as the nervous system's best attempt to help you survive experiences you were too young, too unsupported, or too overwhelmed to process.

The ego is somatic before it is psychological. It is the tightening that helped you endure fear. The numbness that shielded you from pain. The vigilance that kept you from feeling alone. The shrinking that kept you from being hurt. The performance that kept you accepted.

Every egoic pattern began as an act of care — primitive, instinctive care. The body said: *Let me hold this for you. Let me protect you from feeling this too soon.*

Somatic innocence means recognizing that every contraction, every identity, every defensive strategy was born in a moment when your system was doing the best it could. The ego stepped in to carry the weight of an emotion you could not carry yourself. It built walls around the heart not to imprison you, but to keep you safe. It closed the throat not to silence you, but to prevent exposure. It kept you small not to limit your life, but to shield your system from overwhelm.

The ego was not the source of your suffering — it was the way your body tried to prevent more. This is why shame about the ego is unnecessary and harmful. There is nothing shameful about adapting. There is nothing wrong with the survival strategies that kept you intact. There is nothing unspiritual about the body doing what it needed to do.

Somatic innocence reframes the entire awakening process. It shows us that healing is not about attacking the ego, transcending the ego, or dismantling the ego through force. The ego cannot be wrestled out of existence because it is not resisting you — it is trying to protect you. To fight it is to fight the part of you that once saved you.

The ego softens not when judged, but when understood. Not when pushed, but when held. Not when condemned, but when met with compassion.

And as the ego feels this compassion — somatically, not intellectually — it begins to release. The tightness unwinds. The vigilance relaxes. The heart opens. The breath deepens. The self-protective patterns lose their urgency because the nervous system senses that the conditions are finally different: *You are no longer alone. You are no longer unsafe. You no longer need this protection.* This is the moment innocence reveals itself: the realization that the ego was never your prison, it was your guardian.

When you see this, the relationship with your own inner life changes. The parts of you that once felt like burdens begin to feel like younger versions of you, still holding the weight of unprocessed moments. And when these parts are met with presence rather than pressure, they begin to let go — not because you force them to, but because they finally can.

Somatic innocence is the doorway to true release. It is the recognition that the false self was the body's attempt at love. And when love returns — through awareness, presence, or divine safety — the ego no longer has to protect who you are. It can finally rest.

Letting the Old Identity Dissolve Safely

The dissolution of identity is not a dramatic spiritual event — it is a gentle somatic unwinding. The old identity does not fall away because we reject it, transcend it, or forcibly detach from it. It dissolves when the body feels safe enough to release the contractions that once held it together. The ego does not die; it relaxes. The self does not disappear; it expands. And this expansion can only happen when dissolution happens in safety.

Safety is the key. Not insight. Not effort. Not willpower. Safety. The old identity is a survival structure. It was built to protect you from experiences the nervous system could not handle at the time. It held your emotional world together when you lacked the capacity or support to feel what was happening. It is not fragile — it is loyal. And because of that loyalty, it will not dissolve until it senses that you can stand without it.

Letting the old identity dissolve safely begins with honouring it:

- honouring the contractions that once shielded you
- honouring the vigilance that kept you aware
- honouring the perfectionism, the pleasing, the avoidance, the withdrawal — all the ways your younger self learned to survive a world that felt too big

You cannot release what you judge. You cannot dissolve what you shame. You cannot outgrow what you refuse to understand.

The nervous system relaxes only when it feels held — by your awareness, your compassion, your presence. This internal holding replaces the external holding that was missing when the identity formed. And once the body feels supported from within, the old identity no longer has to guard the system. It begins to soften, to loosen its structure, to release its grip.

This dissolution is not linear. It unfolds in waves. Tightness releases. Emotion rises. Breath deepens. Old stories lose their emotional weight. Behaviour patterns feel less compelling. The sense of "me" becomes more spacious.

You begin to notice that the identity you once defended is no longer solid. It feels like a memory, a familiar outfit that no longer fits your shape. You may still reach for it in moments of stress — but it slips off more easily, because the body is no longer contorted into its form.

Letting the old identity dissolve safely means allowing this process to happen at the nervous system's pace, not the mind's.

It means trusting the body's timing. It means recognizing that each release is a return, not a loss. It means sensing that what is falling away is not who you are, but who you had to be.

As the identity dissolves, what emerges is not emptiness, but truth. Not confusion, but clarity. Not vulnerability, but presence. Not loss of self, but the end of self-contraction.

This is how the false self dissolves safely — not through force, but through support; not through pushing, but through opening; not through disconnection, but through deeper connection with the body's intelligence.

And as this gentle unwinding continues, a new way of being emerges: one rooted not in survival, but in coherence; not in contraction, but in openness; not in fear, but in the spaciousness of your true nature.

Letting the old identity dissolve safely is the beginning of returning to who you were before the body learned to protect itself — a return to presence, to authenticity, to the unconditioned self beneath the layers of survival.

When the Self You Built Makes Room for the Self You Are

Trauma does not just touch the mind — it shapes the body, and through the body, it shapes the self. In this chapter, we explored how unresolved emotions form personality, how the "small self" emerges as a survival architecture, why the ego clings to familiar contraction, and how somatic innocence reframes the ego not as an obstacle but as a protector. We saw that identity itself is not a fixed truth but a tension pattern — a constellation of adaptive responses held in muscle, breath, and nervous system memory.

The great unfolding is this: identity is not who you are — it is who you became when you could not yet be yourself. Every pattern, every survival strategy, every contraction was an act of care. The false self was never false in its intention — it was a bridge. A temporary structure built so the system could endure what it wasn't yet ready to fully feel.

And because identity is rooted in the body, its dissolution must also occur through the body. Not through mental insight. Not through disidentification alone. Not through spiritual bypass or conceptual clarity. It dissolves through safety. Through presence. Through awareness entering the very places where identity once contracted.

Letting the old identity dissolve safely is not a stripping away — it is a softening. A melting. A quiet return. What falls away are the protections that once served you but now compress you. What remains is the part of you that contraction obscured: spaciousness, clarity, authenticity, and a deeper intelligence not shaped by fear.

The truth revealed in this chapter is both tender and liberating. When the survival self no longer has to guard the system, the authentic self finally has room to emerge.

This emergence is not the creation of a new identity — it is the remembrance of your original nature. A nature unburdened by shame. Untethered from fear. Unrestricted by the narrow boundaries of the ego. A nature that experiences life directly rather than through the filter of protection.

As we move forward, the path deepens from recognizing how identity forms to understanding how resistance dissolves. Chapter 9 will explore the somatic mechanisms through which fear, control, and contraction unwind — revealing how the body transitions from survival to openness, and how surrender becomes the nervous system's new baseline.

Chapter

9

Dissolving Resistance, Fear, and Control

Why the Nervous System Fears Openness

Openness is our natural state, yet for a nervous system shaped by overwhelm, unpredictability, and unmet emotional experience, openness feels like danger. Not metaphorically — physiologically. The body reads openness not as expansion, but as exposure. Not as freedom, but as vulnerability. Not as possibility, but as the very conditions under which it once felt unprotected and alone.

This fear of openness is not irrational; it is encoded memory. When a child opens — emotionally, energetically, relationally — and the environment does not meet that openness with attunement or safety, the body learns a painful truth:

- *openness leads to hurt*
- *openness leads to overwhelm*
- *openness leads to disconnection*
- *openness leads to shame*

And so, the nervous system closes. It tightens. It narrows its emotional bandwidth. It contracts the breath, guards the heart, and restricts the flow of awareness. Over time, closedness feels like safety. Openness feels like risk.

This is why the body instinctively resists healing — even when the mind is ready for transformation. Openness invites sensation. Sensation invites emotion. Emotion invites vulnerability. And vulnerability is exactly what the nervous system was once unable to handle.

So the nervous system equates openness with the return of past overwhelm. It confuses *then* with *now.* It sees expansion and believes contraction is necessary. It senses spaciousness and activates protection.

This is why people fear joy, intimacy, love, abundance, or visibility just as intensely as they fear conflict or pain. It is not the experience itself they fear — it is the openness required to receive it.

Openness requires:

- allowing sensation
- trusting flow
- releasing control
- letting the heart be accessible
- letting the moment be felt fully
- not knowing what will come next

To a dysregulated nervous system, these conditions mimic the environment of early emotional threat. Openness feels like stepping into the same space where the original wound occurred. The body remembers. And the body protects.

The nervous system fears openness because openness is the opposite of every survival strategy it learned. If your safety once depended on staying small, staying hidden, staying tense, staying vigilant — then expansion feels life-threatening, even if it is exactly what you need.

This is why spiritual openings can be destabilizing. The body is asked to inhabit a level of spaciousness it never associated with safety. The nervous system must unlearn its old conclusions before it can relax into the truth that openness is not danger — it is the return to your natural state.

Openness becomes safe only when the body feels:

- held
- supported
- regulated
- attuned
- accompanied
- resourced from within

Without these conditions, openness feels like falling. With them, it feels like freedom.

Awakening requires this essential shift; moving from a body that fears openness to a body that trusts it; from a nervous system organized around protection to one organized around presence.

As openness becomes tolerable, then safe, then effortless, the entire architecture of the false self begins to dissolve. And what emerges in its place is the expansive, unguarded awareness that has been waiting beneath the layers of contraction all along.

The Body's Attachment to Predictability

The body craves predictability not because it fears change, but because predictability feels like safety. For a nervous system shaped by overwhelm, inconsistency, or emotional unpredictability, the familiar — even if painful — becomes preferable to the unknown. Predictability creates a sense of control, and control creates the illusion that nothing unexpected can break through the system's fragile equilibrium.

This attachment is not psychological — it is physiological. The nervous system is constantly assessing risk. It scans for cues of safety or threat, not based on logic, but based on patterns it has learned through experience. If unpredictability once brought emotional pain, chaos, or harsh consequences, the body encodes a clear conclusion:

- *If I can anticipate, I can protect myself.*
- *If I can control, I can survive.*

Predictability becomes synonymous with stability. Routine becomes synonymous with regulation. The known becomes synonymous with safety. This is why the body clings to old patterns even when they cause suffering. Why it repeats the same relational dynamics. Why it returns to the same emotional loops. Why it prefers familiar contraction over unfamiliar openness. The body would rather stay in a predictable tension than risk an unpredictable freedom.

Change — even positive change — requires the nervous system to enter territory it cannot map. Openness, intimacy, abundance, visibility, joy, and presence all invite experiences that cannot be controlled, rehearsed, or guaranteed. To a nervous system designed around predictability, these states feel like stepping into a space where survival strategies no longer apply.

This is why resistance appears exactly at the threshold of growth. The moment possibility expands, the body contracts. The moment life becomes unpredictable in a good way, the old self panics. The moment openness invites transformation, the nervous system clings to what it already knows. Predictability allows the body to prepare. Openness requires the body to trust.

For someone whose early environment lacked relational steadiness, predictability becomes a lifeline. The brain associates sameness with safety because sameness meant fewer surprises, fewer emotional storms, fewer shocks to the system. Even boredom can feel safer than expansion, because boredom is predictable.

This attachment to predictability shapes identity in subtle ways:

- The *overthinker* tries to predict outcomes to avoid disappointment.
- The *controller* manages details to prevent chaos.
- The *perfectionist* eliminates variables to avoid criticism.
- The *avoider* withdraws to reduce unpredictable emotional impact.
- The *people-pleaser* adapts to others to keep the environment stable.

These identities emerge not from personality, but from the nervous system's devotion to maintaining predictability at all costs.

But predictability, while comforting, is also constricting. It keeps us in loops. It keeps us small. It keeps us from experiencing the fullness of life. And yet, the solution is not to push the body into spontaneity or force it into uncertainty. That only triggers more contraction.

The body loosens its attachment to predictability when it feels resourced enough to handle change. When awareness is present. When connection is felt. When safety is internalized. When openness is introduced gently, not suddenly.

The more supported the nervous system feels, the more it can tolerate the unknown. The more it can let go of control. The more it can allow life to move without bracing.

Predictability stops being the anchor when the body finds a deeper anchor — presence. And as the body learns to trust presence over predictability, resistance dissolves and freedom becomes possible.

This is the transition from survival to embodiment: the shift from a life built on patterns of protection to a life lived from the open intelligence of awareness.

Releasing the Need to Control Experience

Control is not a mindset — it is a somatic strategy. It is the body's attempt to create safety by managing, predicting, or shaping experience before it can become overwhelming. Control is what the nervous system learned when life felt too big, too fast, or too unpredictable. It is not a flaw or a failing; it is a protective reflex. And like all protective reflexes, it hardens into identity when it is repeated long enough.

The need to control arises when the body doesn't trust that it can handle what might come. It is fear wearing the disguise of responsibility. It is vulnerability wrapped in tension. It is overwhelm expressed as hyper-management of reality.

Control feels necessary because the nervous system still lives in the past. It responds to the present moment with the memory of earlier unpredictability. It braces against the future as if the old pain might return at any time. It tries to stay one step ahead of life to avoid being blindsided again.

This is why control shows up most intensely in the areas where we feel most vulnerable — relationships, intimacy, expression, success, visibility, emotions. The body learned:

- *If I can control this, I won't be hurt.*
- *If I can control them, I won't be abandoned.*
- *If I can control myself, I won't be shamed.*
- *If I can control the outcome, I won't be overwhelmed.*

But control does not create safety — it creates contraction:

- it freezes spontaneity
- it limits receiving
- it restricts intuition
- it blocks connection
- it suppresses emotion
- it shrinks awareness

The more we try to control experience, the more life feels like something to manage rather than something to participate in.

Releasing the need to control is not something you *do* — it is something that happens when the body begins to trust the moment again. Trust emerges when the nervous system is regulated. When awareness is present. When the body feels held — by yourself, by others, by Source. When it realizes that the conditions that required control no longer exist.

Control melts in the presence of safety. This release comes in waves:

- a breath deepens
- the shoulders soften
- the belly relaxes
- the mind pauses its scanning
- emotion moves without being suppressed
- sensation is allowed to unfold
- the body opens to life rather than bracing against it

In these moments, the nervous system learns something revolutionary: I can be here without managing this. I can feel this without being overwhelmed. I can allow this without losing myself. As the body integrates this truth, the grip of control loosens naturally.

- You do not lose your capacity for discernment — you lose the tension that made discernment feel like vigilance.
- You do not lose responsibility — you lose the burden of hyper-responsibility that came from fear.
- You do not lose agency — you lose the false agency created by trying to control what was never yours to hold.

Releasing control is not an act of letting go — it is an act of remembering:

- Remembering that openness is possible.
- Remembering that safety is available.
- Remembering that life does not need to be micromanaged.
- Remembering that presence, not control, is what truly stabilizes you.

As the need to control dissolves, a new way of being emerges — one marked by trust, fluidity, and an intimacy with the moment that control could never create. This is the doorway to deeper surrender and the beginning of embodied freedom.

How Surrender Arises Somatically

Surrender is not a choice the mind makes — it is a state the body enters. It is not an act of will, but the natural consequence of a nervous system that no longer feels the need to protect itself. Surrender does not happen because we decide to "let go." It happens because the body realizes, often for the first time, that letting go is safe.

Somatic surrender begins in the exact opposite place the ego expects: not in control, but in softening. Not in effort, but in presence. Not in pushing, but in allowing.

It happens when something inside loosens — a grip, a tension, a vigilance, a boundary we didn't even know we were holding. This softening opens a small space, and through that space, the possibility of surrender enters.

The body does not surrender all at once. It surrenders in micro-movements:

- a breath that drops lower into the belly
- a chest that stops bracing against emotion
- a jaw that unclenches
- a diaphragm that begins to move
- a heart that feels safe enough to open one more degree
- a moment where awareness stays present instead of fleeing

These subtle shifts are not symbolic — they are somatic. Each one signals to the nervous system, *It is safe to let go a little more.* Over time, these small openings accumulate, and the system learns a new pattern: openness without collapse, vulnerability without danger, presence without fear.

This is the physiology of surrender. Surrender also arises when the nervous system trusts the environment — whether that environment is another person, a spiritual field, or the internal presence of awareness itself. When the body senses holding, support, and resonance, it stops preparing for impact. It no longer needs to predict or guard. And without guarding, tension melts. Breath deepens. The body yields.

The ego interprets surrender as loss — loss of control, loss of certainty, loss of protection. But the body experiences surrender as relief:

- relief from hypervigilance
- relief from the exhausting task of managing everything
- relief from bracing against imaginary futures

- relief from carrying the emotional weight of the past

This relief is the nervous system recognizing that it does not need to fight the moment.

Somatic surrender is the shift from *holding life* to *being held by life.* From *resisting experience* to *allowing experience.* From *narrowing awareness* to *expanding into awareness.* It is the moment the survival self steps aside because the system realizes it is no longer required.

And the deeper truth is this: Surrender arises *after* safety, not before. A dysregulated nervous system cannot surrender — it can only submit or collapse. A regulated nervous system surrenders because it feels supported enough to open.

Somatic surrender is not passive. It is receptive. It is not resignation. It is trust. It is not giving up. It is giving in — to presence, to truth, to the deeper intelligence moving through you.

As surrender becomes embodied, awareness expands into spaces the ego once guarded. Life begins to flow through the body rather than being filtered through protection. And the self that emerges is not smaller or weaker — it is freer.

Surrender is the final release of the need to manage the moment, and the first step into the natural state of being that was always waiting beneath the layers of control.

Openness as the New Baseline

Openness is not a peak state — it is the nervous system's natural resting point once fear, resistance, and control have softened. It is the body's original blueprint, the state it always intended to live in before contraction became its default. When openness becomes the new baseline, life no longer feels like something to brace against. It becomes something to meet, to receive, to participate in fully.

Openness is not fragility — it is capacity:

- The capacity to feel without being overwhelmed.
- The capacity to respond without collapsing into old patterns.
- The capacity to remain present even when emotion moves.
- The capacity to stay grounded while also being undefended.

When openness becomes the baseline, the nervous system no longer prepares for threat in the absence of threat. The body no longer scans for danger in moments of calm. The mind no longer rehearses worst-case scenarios to maintain a sense of control. Instead, the system reorganizes itself around safety, coherence, and presence.

This shift is not theoretical — it is physiological. Openness expresses itself through:

- a breath that moves freely through the torso
- a chest that stays soft and available
- a belly that is no longer clenched
- a throat that remains open during expression
- eyes that can relax into connection
- awareness that expands instead of constricts

The body is no longer holding itself in survival. It is inhabiting the moment in real time.

This openness is not the absence of challenge, nor the absence of emotion. It is the absence of *resistance* to challenge and emotion. When openness stabilizes, emotion moves without becoming identity. Experience flows without becoming threat. Sensation rises without triggering bracing. Life feels less like something that happens to you and more like something that happens within you.

Openness as the new baseline changes how you relate to everything:

- Relationships feel easier because you are no longer protecting yourself from connection.
- Receiving becomes natural because the body is no longer braced against vulnerability.
- Expression flows because the throat and heart are no longer constricted.
- Intuition strengthens because the system is no longer cluttered with fear signals.
- Awareness expands because contraction no longer narrows perception.

You begin to live from your actual self, not the self shaped by protection.

This transformation does not occur through insight alone. It happens as the nervous system relearns safety — first in small moments, then in longer stretches, and eventually as the underlying tone of your being. Openness becomes the baseline when the body trusts the present moment more than it trusts the old strategies designed to manage it.

Over time, openness feels like home. The identity that once clung to contraction fades. The reflex to tighten dissolves. The pull toward control softens. The fear of expansion evaporates. The effort to manage life gives way to the ability to *feel* life.

Openness becomes effortless because resistance is no longer necessary. Openness becomes sustainable because safety has been restored. Openness becomes natural because it always was.

When openness stabilizes as the new baseline, awakening stops being a peak state and becomes your way of being. Presence becomes your nervous system's default setting. And life can finally be lived from the spaciousness of who you truly are, rather than the contraction of who you had to be.

When Protection Ends, Presence Begins

Resistance, fear, and control were never defects in your consciousness — they were the body's intelligent attempts to keep you safe. They formed in moments when openness was too much, when unpredictability was overwhelming, when vulnerability felt dangerous. Your system learned to contract because contraction was what kept you intact. And for a long time, it worked.

But what once protected you eventually confined you. What once helped you survive began to limit your capacity to live. What once created safety began to block connection, expression, intimacy, and truth.

In this chapter, we explored why the nervous system fears openness, why it clings to predictability, how control becomes a somatic strategy, and how surrender arises naturally once the body feels safe. We saw how openness — the state we long for — is not something the mind can force, but something the body returns to when protective patterns dissolve. The deeper understanding is this: Awakening is not the victory of willpower; it is the relaxation of protection.

Resistance dissolves not because we fight it, but because we stop needing it. Fear dissolves not because we overpower it, but because we feel supported enough to release it. Control dissolves not because we convince ourselves to “let go,” but because the body finally trusts the moment.

This chapter reveals a path of profound compassion: a recognition that everything you once judged as weakness was actually your system caring for you the only way it knew how.

- When we honour the body’s history of protection, it becomes willing to open.
- When we meet fear with presence, it becomes willingness.
- When we stop shaming resistance, it becomes curiosity.
- When we create safety, surrender becomes natural.

And when surrender becomes natural, openness becomes inevitable.

This is the threshold where the identity shaped by survival softens, and the Self shaped by awareness begins to emerge. Not as a concept, but as a lived experience. Not as something to reach for, but as something that arises when the body is no longer bracing against life.

The chapter closes with this truth: You do not need to force your way into awakening. You need to create the conditions in which your system no longer needs to resist it.

When protection ends, presence begins. And presence — felt through the body, grounded in safety, and infused with awareness — is the foundation on which the rest of your awakening will unfold.

IV

Returning to Oneness Through the Body

Chapter

10

Non-Dual Awakening as Somatic Unity

Non-Duality Explained Somatically, Not Philosophically

Non-duality is often spoken of as a metaphysical principle, a philosophical stance, or an abstract truth about the absence of separation. But none of that touches the living reality of it. Philosophy can point toward oneness, yet the body is where the illusion of separation is actually held — and therefore where oneness must be remembered. Non-duality becomes real not when the mind understands unity, but when the body stops bracing against life.

Every contraction in the nervous system is a small assertion of "me" against the world. Every subtle tightening is the body's way of saying, *I must manage this; I am separate from what is arising.* From this physiological stance, separation feels true long before it becomes a belief. The ego is simply the story the mind tells to explain the body's defensive posture. Thus, the illusion of duality does not originate in thought — it is born in sensation.

This is why awakening cannot be thought into existence. The mind can agree with non-dual teachings while the body remains frozen in old survival patterns. It can repeat spiritual ideas while still contracting around fear, shame, uncertainty, or the need to control experience. The body's tension becomes the unspoken confession: "I know unity in theory, but I do not yet feel safe enough to live it."

When the body finally relaxes, something extraordinary is revealed. As the bracing softens, the boundary between "self" and "other" becomes less defined. Sensations that once seemed personal begin to unfold in a larger field of awareness. The nervous system, no longer scanning for danger, becomes permeable to presence. This permeability is not a mystical metaphor — it is a physiological transition from guardedness to openness, from survival to Being.

In this openness, non-duality stops being a concept and becomes a somatic reality. You begin to notice that awareness is not *inside* the body; rather, the body is arising *within* awareness. The sense of a separate "me" starts to dissolve not because you adopted a new philosophy, but because the felt boundaries that maintained the illusion of separation have relaxed. Spaciousness becomes embodied. Presence becomes tangible. Life is no longer something you experience from behind an internal wall — it moves through you, with you, as you.

This is the heart of somatic non-duality: the recognition that awakening is not an escape from the body but the softening of everything in the body that once obscured unity. When contraction falls away, what remains is not an enlightened idea but a lived intimacy with existence itself. You feel yourself as the space in which life unfolds, no longer divided from it. This unity is not achieved — it is uncovered, revealed when the body no longer needs to defend the illusion of separateness.

Non-duality becomes real the moment the body stops insisting on two.

How the Body Reflects Unity When it Relaxes

When the body relaxes, it reveals truths the mind has been trying to understand for years. Relaxation is not merely the absence of tension — it is the dissolving of the inner boundary that has been mistaken for "self." The moment the nervous system shifts out of vigilance, the sense of "I am here, and life is out there" begins to fade. The body, once organized around survival, reorganizes around openness, coherence, and connection. In this openness, unity stops being a spiritual aspiration and becomes a felt reality.

Relaxation allows the body to return to its natural rhythm, a rhythm that is fundamentally relational. Breath deepens on its own, not because you direct it, but because the body no longer fears the fullness of life entering it. Muscles soften without instruction, as if they finally remember they were never meant to hold the world. The heart begins to radiate warmth and receptivity, not as an emotional performance but as the organic expression of a system no longer defending itself.

What you call "relaxation" is, in truth, the body remembering unity. As the body relaxes, awareness is no longer fragmented. Sensations are no longer interpreted as threats or problems to solve — they are simply movements of life appearing within the same field of consciousness. You feel less like a separate observer and more like the space in which everything is happening. Sounds, sensations, emotions, and the environment no longer feel distant; they arise as part of a single, seamless experience.

This shift is subtle but profound: instead of being *in* your body, you begin to feel that your body is *within* a larger awareness that includes everything else. The edges blur. The sense of separation softens. The nervous system, once contracted into a personal identity, begins to vibrate in harmony with the larger field. Relaxation reveals that unity is somatic, not conceptual.

Even the way you move changes. When the body relaxes, movement becomes fluid, unforced, and connected. There is no longer a "doer" pushing life forward. Action arises naturally, the way a wave rises in the ocean — not separate from its source, but an expression of it. In this state, relational interactions shift as well. You feel others not as objects outside you but as extensions of the same field of presence. Compassion becomes effortless. Listening becomes natural. Intimacy becomes safe.

The body reflects unity most clearly in its ease. A relaxed body does not confirm the illusion of separation; it reveals the underlying reality of oneness. It shows that the world is not attacking you, life is not pushing against you, and you do not need to brace to exist. You are already held by something larger, something that includes everything you meet.

When the body relaxes, unity is no longer something you reach for — it is something you finally stop resisting.

Oneness as a Felt Experience Rather than Belief

Oneness becomes real the moment it is felt, not the moment it is understood. Belief can gesture toward unity, but it cannot deliver the lived intimacy of it. You can tell yourself that all is one, that separation is illusion, that consciousness is indivisible — yet if your body is tense, defended, bracing, or contracted, you will continue to *feel* like a separate self navigating a world of others. Belief is a mental agreement; unity is a somatic revelation.

This is why genuine awakening does not begin with adopting a spiritual framework — it begins when the body becomes safe enough to stop resisting the present moment. As long as survival physiology is active, the nervous system will interpret life through the lens of "self-versus-world." But when the body softens, something deeper emerges: a direct, unmistakable sensation of being woven into the fabric of everything around you.

Oneness is not a philosophy you hold. It is a texture you feel. It might appear as an unexpected spaciousness spreading through the chest, an ease in the belly, or a quiet stillness behind the heart. It might arise as the sense that breath is not something "you" are doing, but something happening through you, as part of a larger rhythm. It might reveal itself as the dissolving of the subtle line between "my energy" and "the environment," a sense of permeability that feels both peaceful and intimate.

In these moments, you are no longer relating to life — you are immersed in it. The mind may try to interpret this as a mystical or altered state, but it is simply the body returning to its natural coherence. Unity is the default state once contraction is absent. Nothing needs to be added; only the illusion of separation needs to fall away. And it falls away not through insight, but through the body's gradual unwinding of old protective patterns.

As the body relaxes into presence, the felt-sense of "I" begins to expand. Instead of identifying with a single point inside the skin, awareness feels spacious, inclusive, and boundaryless. You experience yourself as the field in which everything arises — sounds, sensations, movements, other people, the environment. There is no longer an inner world and an outer world; there is one unfolding experience happening within the same vastness.

This lived unity is unmistakable. It does not depend on belief, effort, or spiritual language. It is self-evident, as natural as the warmth of sunlight on your skin. You feel connected without trying. You feel open without effort. You feel whole without striving for transcendence.

Oneness becomes real not through understanding, but through the nervous system's return to openness. When the body settles, awareness becomes unbound, and life is no longer experienced from the perspective of a separate self. You discover that unity was not something to achieve — it was what you were already immersed in, once the contractions of separation dissolved.

Awareness, Sensation, and the Dissolving Boundary

The boundary between "self" and "world" is not primarily a thought — it is a sensation. It is the felt sense of being enclosed, separate, or contained within the body. It is the subtle tightening around experience that gives rise to the impression that awareness is happening *inside* you, while life is happening *outside* you. When the body constricts, this boundary feels solid. When the body relaxes, the boundary begins to thin. And when awareness fully opens to sensation, the boundary dissolves entirely.

Awareness and sensation were never meant to be two. Awareness is the space in which sensation appears; sensation is the expression of awareness in form. The illusion of separation arises only when awareness collapses into a narrow point of identification — when it believes itself to be the body rather than the field that perceives the body. But as awareness expands and becomes intimate with sensation rather than resisting it, a remarkable shift occurs: sensation stops feeling personal. Instead of "my" sensation, it becomes simply "this" sensation — arising within the boundless field of presence that you are.

This is the beginning of the dissolving boundary. When awareness meets sensation without fear, without avoidance, without clinging or analysis, the nervous system softens. The protective shell around experience loosens. The body no longer needs to hold sensation as something threatening or private. Awareness becomes spacious enough to include everything it once tried to manage. Slowly, the internal world and the external world merge.

You begin to notice that the same field of awareness that perceives sensation in your chest is the field that perceives the sound of a bird, the movement of air on your skin, the presence of another person in the room. Awareness does not stop at the edge of the body; it flows through it, around it, beyond it. Sensation, once experienced as something happening "to me," becomes part of the larger tapestry of existence arising in a single, unified field.

When awareness fully embraces sensation, the body is no longer the boundary of identity — it is just another expression within the whole.

This is not dissociation or detachment; it is the most intimate form of presence. You feel more, not less. You sense life with greater depth, clarity, and softness. The difference is that nothing feels separate. Sensation is not an interruption of awareness — it is the texture of awareness itself.

In this union, the nervous system reorganizes around openness. The bracing that once defined the self naturally dissolves. Sensations that once triggered defence now unfold freely. Even emotional waves lose their solidity when held in open awareness; they move through like currents, not identities.

The dissolving boundary is not a mystical event — it is the body remembering its original coherence with everything it touches, perceives, and includes. Awareness expands, sensation softens, and the line that once divided "me" from "life" disappears into a spacious presence that holds all of it.

Unity is revealed when nothing in your experience needs to be excluded, protected against, or kept separate.

Internal and External Merging Into Presence

As the boundary between awareness and sensation dissolves, something even more fundamental begins to shift: the division between the "internal" world and the "external" world loses its meaning. What once felt like two realms — an inner landscape of thoughts, emotions, and sensations, and an outer landscape of people, objects, and events — begins to reveal itself as one continuous field of presence. This merging is not the result of effort or spiritual technique; it emerges naturally when the nervous system no longer contracts around the idea of separateness.

Chapter 10

The sense of an inner world is maintained by tension. When the body braces, awareness narrows and folds inward, creating the impression of something private, personal, contained. Likewise, the sense of an external world is created by the feeling of pushing against something other, something outside your skin, something that must be managed or defended against. But when the body relaxes out of survival mode, these orientations lose their structure. The body no longer feels like a container — it feels like an openness through which life flows.

Presence, in this state, becomes the meeting point of all experience. Not a place inside you, not a place around you, but the unified field in which both arise.

Thoughts appear not as internal monologues but as gentle movements within the same awareness that holds the sound of wind or the sight of another person's face. Emotional waves rise within the same space in which trees sway or a room brightens with sunlight. Sensation in the chest is felt within the same vastness that perceives the world. Everything is arising in one place — presence.

This merging is not abstract or conceptual. It is felt directly, somatically. You may notice moments where your breath feels connected to the rhythm of the environment, as if the inhalation is drawn from the space around you and the exhalation dissolves back into it. You may sense another person not as separate, but as a movement of the same presence expressing itself through a different form. The distinction between "my aliveness" and "the aliveness of the world" becomes thinner, softer, more permeable — eventually disappearing altogether.

In this merging, there is no longer a you perceiving the world; there is only perception itself. There is no longer an inner state and an outer circumstance; there is only the unfolding of experience within presence. And because this presence is inherently unified, conflict loses its anchor. Resistance has no foothold. Control becomes irrelevant. Everything is allowed to arise exactly as it is, and everything is included in the vastness that you are.

You become life experiencing itself from within itself. This is the essence of somatic non-duality — not the erasure of the body, but the recognition that the body is one expression of the same presence that forms the trees, the sky, the breath, the heartbeat, the movement of others, and the stillness behind all things. Internal and external merge into a single experiential field, not through transcendence, but through deep relaxation into the truth that was always here.

When presence becomes the ground of both worlds, awakening shifts from an idea to a way of being. Nothing is outside you, and nothing is separate from the awareness through which it is known. This is unity lived through the body — the remembering that all of life is happening in one continuous now, held by one continuous consciousness, expressed through one continuous field of being.

The Softening Into Everything

Non-dual awakening does not arrive as a grand revelation from above but as a gentle softening from within. It enters through the body, through the places where you stop resisting, where you allow yourself to be felt by life instead of bracing against it. The more the body relaxes, the more the illusion of separation dissolves. What once appeared as an isolated “me” reveals itself to be a wave within a larger ocean — distinct in shape, but inseparable in essence.

The journey of this chapter has pointed again and again to a simple truth: unity is not achieved; it is uncovered. It is revealed when you stop clinging to the survival patterns that once kept you small and separate. It emerges when awareness meets sensation with tenderness instead of fear. It deepens when the boundary between inner and outer loses its solidity and experience becomes one continuous expression unfolding in presence.

Non-dual awakening is not something you learn. It is something your body remembers. The more you rest into this remembering, the more natural it becomes to live without dividing life into parts — without splitting your experience into inside and outside, self and other, spiritual and ordinary. Unity begins to permeate everything: your relationships, your decisions, your breath, your movements, your sense of identity. Life becomes less about seeking connection and more about relaxing into the connection that has always been here.

As the bracing softens and presence takes its rightful place, you discover a state beyond striving — a quiet intimacy with existence itself. You are no longer trying to merge with the whole; you are noticing that you never left it. The body becomes a vessel for this recognition, not an obstacle to it. Its sensations, once interpreted as evidence of separation, become gateways into the lived truth of oneness.

Non-dual awakening is ultimately the effortless realization that you are not a fragment observing the world, but the field in which the world appears. The end of separation is not an attainment but a return — a return to the original openness that has held you from the beginning.

This is the softening into everything. This is unity remembered through the body.

Chapter

11

The Heart as the Bridge Between Form and Awareness

The Heart Field and Somatic Coherence

The heart is not simply an emotional centre — it is the body's deepest point of contact with awareness itself. Long before the mind forms interpretations, long before the nervous system organizes itself around protection or habit, the heart is already registering reality directly. It is sensing, attuning, resonating. It is responding to life not through cognition but through a quiet, undeniable intelligence that arises from presence. When we speak of the heart as the bridge between form and awareness, we are pointing to this deeper truth: the heart is the first place in the body where separation softens and coherence becomes possible.

Somatic coherence is not a technique, nor is it something we manufacture through effort. It is what naturally emerges when the layers of contraction that obscure the heart begin to loosen. In that softening, the body stops defending against life. The breath deepens without instruction. The chest expands without force. And the subtle field around the heart — an energetic atmosphere that extends beyond the physical body — begins to harmonize with the larger field of awareness that holds all things. This coherence is not emotional positivity or calmness; it is the dissolution of inner conflict. It is the moment the body stops arguing with reality.

When the heart field opens, experience becomes simpler. Sensations that once felt overwhelming now appear as waves moving through a larger ocean of presence. Emotions lose their sharp edges because they are no longer held inside a contracted identity. Instead of being pushed away or analyzed, they are allowed to arise and dissolve within the vastness of the heart. This is why the heart is so central to the somatic path of awakening: it is where the body stops closing around experience and begins letting life flow freely again.

The heart field also has a regulating effect on the rest of the body. It broadcasts safety to the nervous system in a way no thought or affirmation ever could. The parasympathetic system begins to lead. Muscles release because they finally feel they can. The breath becomes unforced, rhythmic, trustworthy. In this coherence, the body remembers its original design — not survival at all costs, but openness as the natural state. What emerges is a deep sense of internal order, a feeling that everything inside you is moving in the same direction, aligned with the same truth.

This coherence is not passive. It is a form of power — not the forceful kind that comes from identity, but the effortless kind that comes from connection. When the heart field is open, awareness is no longer experienced as something distant or abstract. It is embodied. It is felt. It moves through the body the way sunlight moves through water. The heart becomes the transmitter, and the body becomes the instrument through which presence expresses itself.

To live from this coherence is to move through the world without bracing. It is to sense life not from the contracted vantage point of the ego but from the spaciousness of the heart. Clarity arises without struggle. Compassion arises without effort. Love becomes less an emotion and more a state of being that organizes everything from within. In this way, the heart reveals itself as the bridge — the place where the physical dissolves into the infinite, where the personal becomes permeable to the universal, where form remembers its inseparable relationship to awareness.

The path of the heart is not an escape from the body; it is the body opening to its own depth. Through the heart, the body no longer stands apart from awareness — it becomes the field through which awareness knows itself. And in that coherence, awakening moves from being a concept to a lived, intimate reality.

Emotional Transparency as Awakening

Emotional transparency is not the exposure of our inner life to others — it is the exposure of our inner life to **ourselves**. It is the moment the heart stops hiding, stops negotiating with truth, and stops filtering experience through the lens of what feels safe or familiar. Emotional transparency is the felt recognition that nothing arising within us is separate from the field of awareness that holds it. In this way, transparency is not simply honesty; it is awakening revealing itself through the body.

Most of what we call “emotional difficulty” is not the emotion itself but the contraction wrapped around it — the bracing against feeling, the subtle refusal to let something move through, the belief that certain sensations threaten who we are.

Emotional transparency dissolves these layers. It allows sadness to be sadness, anger to be anger, fear to be fear, without collapsing into identity or resistance. The heart no longer tightens around the experience; instead, it becomes spacious enough to let the emotion complete its natural arc.

Transparency is not emotional flooding. It is not catharsis. It is the opposite of overwhelm. It is the clarity that comes when we stop manipulating our emotional reality to maintain an image, protect a narrative, or preserve a sense of control. In transparency, the heart becomes an open environment where experience is free to arise, be known, and dissolve without leaving residue. Nothing is repressed; nothing is dramatized. The inner world becomes unmasked, yet simultaneously held in the quiet intelligence of presence.

As this transparency deepens, emotions lose their charge because they lose their story. What once felt personal becomes simply movement — sensation, energy, life expressing itself through the body. The heart recognizes that nothing appearing within us is a threat. It sees that fear, grief, desire, joy, and tenderness all emerge from the same Source and return to the same spaciousness. Emotional transparency reveals that every emotion is just awareness in motion.

This is why emotional transparency is inseparable from awakening. Awakening is not the absence of emotion; it is the absence of resistance to emotion. It is the end of the inner struggle against what arises. The heart becomes honest not in a performative way but in an energetic way — it stops pretending to be closed. It stops pretending to be separate. It allows life to move through unfiltered and unprotected, trusting that nothing true can be harmed.

In this state, the heart becomes a doorway rather than a barrier. Emotional transparency becomes a form of alignment — a moment-to-moment willingness to remain undefended, receptive, and real. It is not about being "positive" or "spiritual." It is about being present enough to feel life without shrinking away. And through this openness, a profound transformation occurs: the emotional body reorganizes itself around truth rather than fear.

What emerges is a deeper coherence, not because the emotions disappear, but because they no longer distort our perception. They no longer define us, bind us, or dictate our behaviour. They simply pass through the open space of the heart the way wind moves through an uncaged room. In this fluidity, awakening becomes embodied — not a conceptual understanding but a lived transparency where every emotion reveals more of what we truly are.

Emotional transparency is the heart remembering that it has nothing to hide and nothing to protect. It is the beginning of living without inner walls. And in that vulnerability, the bridge between form and awareness becomes unmistakably clear.

Love as the Natural State of a Regulated System

Love is not an emotion we manufacture — it is the baseline of a nervous system that is no longer bracing against life. When the body is regulated, when the heart field is coherent, love arises not as an act of will but as a natural expression of ease. It is what remains when fear drains out of the system, when contraction softens, and when the organism no longer perceives existence as a threat. In this way, love is not something we learn; it is something we uncover by returning the body to its original, unarmored state.

A regulated system does not mean a perfectly calm system. It means a system that can meet experience without collapsing into survival patterns. In that resilience, love becomes the default orientation — not romantic love, not emotional attachment, but the simple, clear openness that recognizes the inherent unity of all experience. Love becomes a physiological spaciousness. It is the felt sense that nothing inside you needs defending and nothing outside you needs controlling.

When the heart is regulated, its field expands. This expansion is not metaphorical; it is somatic. The chest softens. The breath releases. The diaphragm stops holding. The subtle energy around the heart stabilizes into coherence. And within this coherence, the body communicates safety to itself. That safety is what we experience as love. Not idealized, not sentimental — but a grounded acceptance that flows effortlessly from presence.

This is why love cannot be forced. If the nervous system is dysregulated, the heart cannot stay open. The body contracts, the mind tightens, and love becomes an aspiration rather than a lived reality. But as regulation increases, the heart naturally shifts from defence to connection. It becomes easier to breathe around what once felt overwhelming. It becomes possible to stay present with others without losing yourself. It becomes obvious that love is not something you give — it is something you *are* when fear is absent.

A regulated heart recognizes wholeness everywhere. It sees through the illusion of separation not through spiritual philosophy but through direct, embodied knowing. Love becomes the way awareness perceives itself in form. It animates the body with warmth, clarity, and an unforced generosity. It makes presence accessible, compassion effortless, and intimacy safe. In this state, relationships transform because we are no longer relating from a defended identity but from the open clarity of the heart.

As love becomes the natural baseline, life feels less like a series of challenges to overcome and more like a continuous flow of connection. The body begins to trust the moment. The mind begins to quiet. The emotional landscape becomes fluid and alive. And in this fluidity, love expresses itself in countless subtle ways — through patience, through spaciousness, through honesty, through the absence of reactivity, through the quiet willingness to meet reality exactly as it is.

Love, at its core, is the physiological imprint of non-separation. It is what the body feels when the heart is unburdened, when the nervous system is aligned with truth rather than fear. It is the lived signature of unity. And as the system regulates, this love becomes less an experience that comes and goes and more the underlying atmosphere in which all experience arises.

To live from this place is to move through the world with a heart that is not efforting to be open — it simply is. Love becomes the most stable expression of your being, not because you achieved it, but because your system has returned to its natural coherence. In remembering this, the heart completes its role as the bridge between form and awareness, revealing that love was never something to reach for — it was the ground beneath everything all along.

Why the Heart Must Open for Non-Duality to Stabilize

Non-duality may first be recognized in the mind — as insight, as clarity, as a moment where the sense of a separate "me" dissolves into the spaciousness of awareness. But insight alone cannot hold this recognition. The mind can glimpse non-duality, but it cannot *live* it. For non-duality to stabilize, it must descend into the body, soften the contractions that give rise to identity, and ultimately open the heart. The heart is where awakening becomes embodied, coherent, and trustworthy.

When the heart is closed, the body remains organized around protection. Even if the mind recognizes oneness, the nervous system continues to perceive separation. It braces against sensation, filters experience through fear, and interprets life through the lens of threat. In this state, non-dual insight becomes unstable — it flickers, it collapses, it becomes overshadowed by emotional reactivity or old patterns of survival. The heart cannot stay closed and hold unity at the same time. The physiology must match the awareness.

Opening the heart shifts the body out of survival and into connection. This shift is not philosophical; it is somatic. The heart field expands, coherence increases, and the defensive layers that once held the sense of "self" begin to dissolve. The body stops contracting around identity. Emotional waves are allowed to move without being interpreted as danger. The system becomes transparent enough for non-dual awareness to flow through unimpeded. In this openness, unity stops being a realization and becomes a lived reality.

The heart is also the bridge between awareness and form. Without its openness, the mind may detach from life in the name of spirituality, mistaking dissociation for awakening. But when the heart opens, awakening becomes relational — not in terms of dependence, but in terms of presence. You can meet others without losing yourself, and you can meet yourself without retreating into the mind. The heart anchors awareness in the world, allowing non-duality to be expressed through the body rather than used as an escape from it.

This is why the deepest stages of awakening are always accompanied by increasing tenderness. Not sentimentality, but an unmistakable softening — a dissolving of inner rigidity, a willingness to be touched by life. The heart becomes permeable, receptive, undefended. It can feel without collapsing. It can love without clinging. It can experience the full range of human emotion without losing its connection to the vastness that holds it. In this, non-duality becomes stable because nothing arising within experience is pushed away.

When the heart remains closed, separation persists in subtle ways. There is still "me" protecting, "me" navigating, "me" withholding, "me" interpreting. The heart is where this final layer of selfhood dissolves — the last contraction that keeps awakening fragmented. As the heart opens, the boundary between self and world becomes increasingly transparent. Internal and external begin to merge. Life is no longer happening "to" you or "inside" you; it is arising *as* you, *through* you, and within the same undivided field.

To stabilize non-duality is to allow the heart to become the anchor of your being. It is to let the heart's openness regulate the nervous system, refine perception, and attune you to the inherent unity beneath all experience. It is to recognize that awakening is not complete until love becomes as natural as breath — not sentimental love, but the spacious, clear, unconditional presence that emerges when nothing in you is resisting life.

The heart must open because the heart is where oneness becomes lived. It is where insight becomes embodiment, where awareness becomes intimacy, and where the dissolving of separation becomes a lasting, embodied truth.

Embodied Compassion and Unity Consciousness

Compassion, in its pure form, is not a moral quality — it is the natural expression of a nervous system no longer defended against itself or the world. When the heart opens and the body releases the residues of separation, compassion emerges effortlessly as the way awareness relates to manifestation. It is not something you practice; it is something you *become* as the boundaries that once defined "self" soften into transparency.

Embodied compassion is not sentimental or emotional. It does not depend on liking someone, agreeing with them, or understanding their story. It arises because the heart recognizes itself in all forms. The moment the body lets go of the contraction that says "this is me" and "that is other," compassion becomes the obvious response — not as effort, but as recognition. Unity consciousness is not an idea you believe in; it is the lived experience of no longer feeling separate at the level of sensation.

This form of compassion is grounded, clear, and unreactive. It does not collapse into rescuing or take on the suffering of others. It does not bypass pain or turn away from discomfort. Instead, it sits in the depth of presence and allows life to be exactly as it is. Embodied compassion can hold suffering without absorbing it, meet fear without flinching, and stay open in the presence of another's closed heart. It is spacious enough for all experience because it arises from the same awareness that holds the universe itself.

Unity consciousness begins in the heart, but it is completed in the body. The mind can understand oneness philosophically, but the body must feel it. When the heart field expands into coherence, the sense of "me" and "not me" dissolves in lived experience. You feel the subtle resonance between your own emotional landscape and the emotional landscape of others. You sense that what moves through you is not separate from what moves through the collective. Compassion arises because the heart perceives through unity rather than through identity.

In this state, you no longer relate to others from the surface layer of personality. You sense the innocence beneath their patterns, the fear beneath their defensiveness, the longing beneath their aggression. You intuitively understand that each person is shaped by their nervous system, their history, their held contractions — and that none of these define their essence. Embodied compassion sees beyond behaviour to the deeper truth: everything is an expression of the same awareness learning to recognize itself.

This is not passive acceptance; it is powerful presence. Embodied compassion allows you to remain grounded in your own coherence while offering a field of safety that helps others unwind their own contraction. In unity consciousness, your presence becomes medicine. You do not fix, heal, or intervene — you simply stand as an open heart, and in that openness, others feel themselves without judgment or threat. It is here that transformation happens organically.

As compassion becomes embodied, life begins to feel less like a set of individual experiences and more like a continuous flow of shared existence. The recognition of unity does not remove the uniqueness of form; it reveals the seamless field that expresses itself through every form. You move through the world with a heart that is not only open but attuned — sensitive, grounded, and capable of meeting each moment with clarity and warmth.

Embodied compassion and unity consciousness are the final movements of the heart's awakening. They reflect a system that has released the illusion of separateness and now lives from the deeper truth of interconnectedness. To embody compassion is to live as the heart field itself — spacious, coherent, and free — where awareness takes form not as a separate self but as the living presence of love, meeting itself in all things.

The Heart as the Living Threshold of Awakening

The journey of awakening always brings us back to the heart — not as a poetic metaphor, but as the precise somatic doorway through which separation dissolves. The mind can glimpse truth, the nervous system can release its grip, and the body can unwind old patterns, but it is the heart that ultimately integrates awakening into lived experience. The heart is where formless awareness touches form, where presence meets sensation, and where the vastness of consciousness reveals itself as the substance of every moment.

When the heart opens, life stops being something we navigate and becomes something we allow. The armouring that once enclosed identity softens. The stories that shaped our emotional world lose their authority. And the tension that kept us separate from the fullness of our own being releases into a deeper coherence. In this openness, the body is no longer a container for fear but a vessel for presence — a way for awareness to express itself with clarity, compassion, and truth.

Through the heart, non-duality becomes human. Unity becomes relational. Presence becomes tangible. It is in the heart that love shifts from an emotion to a frequency, from a hope to a baseline, from a concept to the very nature of perception itself. The heart does not merely feel love — it becomes the atmosphere in which all experience arises. Everything is met from the same openness, the same transparency, the same willingness to remain unarmoured in the face of life.

This chapter has revealed the heart as more than an emotional centre. It is the bridge through which awakening stabilizes, the field through which compassion naturally emerges, and the intelligence through which the body aligns with the truth of oneness. When the heart is coherent, the nervous system regulates. When the heart is transparent, emotional honesty becomes effortless. When the heart is undefended, love becomes the natural state. And when the heart opens fully, unity consciousness is no longer an insight — it becomes reality lived through flesh and breath.

To walk the somatic path to awakening is to walk through the heart. It is to let the heart field guide perception, to let its coherence regulate the body, and to let its openness dissolve the illusion of separateness. The heart is both the bridge and the destination — the living threshold where form remembers awareness, and awareness remembers itself through form.

In returning to the heart, we return to the deepest truth: we were never separate, only temporarily closed. The heart is the home where awakening becomes whole.

Chapter

12

Sexuality, Intimacy, and the Dissolving of Separation

Sexuality is often one of the most misunderstood dimensions of awakening. For many, it carries layers of conditioning, shame, longing, fear, or confusion — yet at its core, sexuality is simply another expression of life moving through the body. Nothing about this chapter is meant to elevate sexual experience above any other doorway into awakening, nor to suggest that intimacy is required for spiritual growth.

Rather, sexuality is one of many gateways through which the nervous system reveals its patterns of contraction and openness. It offers a uniquely immediate, embodied mirror for sensing where the self still protects, where it still withholds, and where it is ready to soften. In this way, sexuality is not separate from the somatic path — it is simply one context in which the body shows us the truth of our readiness, our vulnerability, and our capacity to receive life fully.

Ego-Driven Intimacy Vs. Heart-Centred Intimacy

Ego-driven intimacy is never truly intimacy. It is proximity shaped by fear, desire, and the nervous system's attempt to secure itself through another body. In this state, we do not meet the other — we meet our own unmet needs, our projections, our compensations, and the somatic patterns that have not yet dissolved. The body tightens, the breath narrows, and the encounter becomes an exchange of survival strategies rather than an expression of presence. Even when the moment appears pleasurable, the underlying field is one of contraction: *Am I desired? Am I safe? Am I enough?* The ego looks for confirmation, validation, and control. It turns intimacy into an attempt to resolve a sense of lack that cannot be fulfilled by another person.

This is why ego-driven intimacy often oscillates between hunger and avoidance, longing and defensiveness. It carries a subtle tension — the fear of being seen and the fear of not being seen, both held at once. The nervous system moves in anticipation rather than in openness. Touch becomes something to manage. Sensation becomes something to brace against. Even connection becomes performance. The ego seeks closeness but fears the vulnerability true closeness demands. And so it reaches for intensity in place of depth, stimulation in place of surrender, fantasy in place of embodied presence.

Heart-centred intimacy emerges only as the body softens out of survival. It arises when the nervous system no longer treats closeness as a threat and the self no longer uses another person to stabilize identity. In this space, we do not enter intimacy to gain anything. We enter because there is nothing left to protect. The heart becomes the meeting point between two beings who are no longer relating from contraction but from openness. Touch becomes an extension of awareness. Sensation becomes a doorway into deeper presence. Connection becomes effortless, not because effort has been perfected, but because defensiveness has dissolved.

In heart-centred intimacy, the body is no longer attempting to grasp, secure, or prove. It is simply allowing. The encounter feels spacious, grounded, and coherent. There is a natural slowness, not imposed but arising from the absence of urgency. Nothing is being taken. Nothing is being extracted. The moment is not a strategy; it is a revelation. Through this openness, intimacy becomes a somatic bridge into unity — a place where we experience the dissolving of boundaries not as a loss, but as a remembering.

When intimacy moves from the heart, the other person is not a means to soothe fragmentation but a mirror of the wholeness already present within. Connection becomes an expression of truth rather than a compensation for separation. The nervous system expands rather than contracts; awareness deepens rather than narrows. What unfolds is not something performed but something revealed. This is intimacy not as escape, but as awakening — where the body, the heart, and consciousness move as one field, and the encounter becomes a practice in dissolving the very separation we once tried to resolve through desire.

Here, union stops being something we seek and becomes something we feel. And in that shift, intimacy transforms from a survival pattern into a sacred opening, guiding the body back into the truth that has always been waiting beneath the ego's grasping: connection is not something we create; it is something we remember.

Physical Intimacy as a Somatic Mirror for Receiving

Physical intimacy reveals, with exquisite precision, how open or closed the nervous system truly is. It mirrors our capacity to receive — not in theory, not in aspiration, but in the felt truth of the body. In sexual connection, every bypass collapses. The body cannot pretend to be open if it is bracing. It cannot fake surrender if it is afraid. It cannot mask contraction with desire. Sexual energy amplifies whatever is present in the system, making intimacy one of the clearest mirrors for where separation still lives within us.

When we enter sexual connection from a contracted state, the encounter becomes an extension of our survival physiology. The body tightens to maintain control. Breath shallowly hovers at the surface. Sensation becomes overwhelming or muted, not because of the experience itself, but because the nervous system is still organized around protection. We may desire closeness, but the body is still negotiating safety. In this state, receiving feels threatening. Pleasure may trigger anxiety. Openness may feel like exposure. And instead of surrendering into sensation, we subtly manage it — tightening, anticipating, performing, or dissociating.

This is where physical intimacy becomes a profound somatic teacher. It shows us where we cannot yet allow life to move through us. It reveals where we still hold back from being touched — not only physically, but emotionally and energetically. It shows the parts of us that believe receiving is dangerous, that vulnerability is too much, that pleasure is not safe, or that being met deeply will demand a self we don't yet know how to inhabit. Through this mirror, we see that difficulty in receiving sexually is not about technique or preference; it is about the nervous system's capacity for openness.

As the body softens out of its survival patterns, something shifts. Receiving stops being an act of effort and becomes an act of allowing. Pleasure no longer feels like too much; it feels like truth. The nervous system, once organized around vigilance, reorganizes around trust. Sensation becomes richer, fuller, more nuanced — not because it is louder, but because the body is no longer suppressing it. The boundaries that once felt rigid begin to dissolve, not through force but through safety. And in this dissolution, receiving becomes natural.

Physical intimacy then becomes a portal, a living demonstration of how the body meets life. If we can receive intimately, we can receive emotionally, creatively, spiritually. If we can allow another to meet us without bracing, we can allow life to meet us without bracing. If we can open in the face of intensity, we can open in the face of possibility. Sexual receiving becomes the training ground for receiving on every level — love, abundance, praise, connection, opportunity, and even awakening itself.

At its highest expression, physical intimacy becomes an embodied practice of surrender, not to another person but to the deeper intelligence moving through both bodies. The encounter becomes less about stimulation and more about coherence. Less about desire and more about presence. Less about performance and more about allowing the natural movement of energy to reveal itself. In this way, sexual intimacy becomes a map of awakening — a mirror showing whether the body is still holding the story of separation or is ready to remember unity.

To receive in physical intimacy is to let the boundary between self and other soften. To let sensation enter without defence. To let the heart open while the body is fully alive. To allow pleasure to dissolve identity. This is why sexual energy is such a potent mirror: it exposes the truth of our capacity to be touched by life itself. And as that capacity grows, physical intimacy transforms from an act into a doorway, guiding us somatically into the dissolving of separation — into the very oneness we have always been longing to remember.

Sexual Energy as the Movement of Source

Sexual energy is not merely a biological impulse; it is the primal movement of life itself — the same force that animates creation, awakens consciousness, and dissolves the illusion of separation. At its core, sexual energy is Source expressing through the body as aliveness, expansion, and the impulse toward union. It is the raw, unfiltered pulse of existence moving through form, seeking not gratification but coherence. When we misunderstand it as something personal or transactional, we collapse its vastness into the narrow frame of egoic desire. But when we meet it with awareness, it becomes unmistakably clear: this energy is the body's most accessible doorway into the truth of oneness.

Sexual energy rises naturally when the system begins to soften out of defence. It flows when the boundaries that once protected us loosen their grip. It reveals itself when we stop contracting against life. In this way, sexual energy becomes a direct indicator of how open we are to Source — not as an idea, but as an embodied current. When the ego attempts to control or suppress this energy, it becomes distorted, reduced to craving, fantasy, or compulsion. The energy still wants to move, but it must move through the tightness of identity, creating tension instead of liberation. We sense the immensity behind it, yet feel unprepared to let it fully touch us.

When the body awakens, however, sexual energy transforms. It shifts from a feeling of pressure to a feeling of expansion. It is no longer something we try to contain or discharge; it becomes something we allow to flow through us with intelligence and grace. The energy moves up as easily as it moves down, circulating through the heart, the spine, the belly, the crown, inviting every layer of us to open. In this state, sexual energy is not localized — it is spacious, luminous, alive. It is the same current we feel in deep meditation, in profound presence, in moments of awe, in unconditional love. It is Source recognizing itself in the body.

Because of this, sexual energy often becomes a catalyst for awakening. It exposes where the self still resists surrender. It illuminates where we cling to control. It invites us into a depth of openness the ego cannot maintain. When this energy rises without narrative — free of grasping or fear — it becomes a somatic revelation: there is no separation between the spiritual and the physical. The body is not an obstacle to awakening; it is an instrument through which awakening becomes felt.

In intimate connection, when two nervous systems are open, this energy begins to move in a field larger than either person. It is not “my” energy or “your” energy but a shared current, arising through two forms yet belonging to neither. The encounter transcends personal desire and becomes a moment of being moved by something greater. Pleasure becomes spacious. Touch becomes prayerful. Breathing becomes synchronized without effort. The sense of “me” dissolves into a widening field of awareness. In these moments, intimacy becomes not the fusion of two selves but the revelation of the one consciousness expressing through both.

This is the true nature of sexual energy: it is Source remembering itself through the body. It is the movement of life reclaiming its fullness. It is the dissolving of edges, the melting of resistance, the softening of identity into pure presence. When we allow this energy to move without fear, it becomes a teacher — showing us how to surrender, how to receive, how to open beyond our conditioning, and how to let the truth of unity be felt rather than merely understood.

Sexual energy, when freed from egoic contraction, is not something we possess. It is something we participate in. It is the pulse of creation moving through us. And as we learn to meet it with awareness, the body becomes a living bridge between form and the infinite — a place where Source flows unobstructed, revealing that the deepest intimacy is not between two people, but between consciousness and its own expression.

Intimacy as a Practice of Somatic Awakening

Intimacy, when entered with awareness, becomes one of the most direct pathways to somatic awakening. It invites the body into territory the mind cannot navigate: openness without control, contact without defence, vulnerability without collapse. In intimacy, the nervous system is asked to do something profound — to remain open in the presence of another being while sensation rises, while emotion stirs, while stories and identities loosen around the edges. This is not merely relational; it is deeply spiritual. Intimacy becomes the space where the body learns to dissolve separation, not conceptually, but through lived experience.

When we approach intimacy unconsciously, we bring the architecture of our survival patterns into the encounter. We brace, even subtly. We anticipate. We monitor the other person's reactions. We manage our own expression. We perform openness rather than inhabit it. These micro-contractions reveal the places where awakening has not yet penetrated the body. The beauty of intimacy is that it makes these patterns unmistakable. What remains hidden in daily life becomes clear in closeness: every flinch, every tightening, every difficulty receiving, every urge to withdraw or grasp, every moment we feel too seen or not seen enough. Intimacy becomes a mirror for where the ego still organizes the nervous system around protection.

But when we approach intimacy as a practice — rather than a possession, an escape, or a negotiation — something shifts. The purpose of the encounter is no longer validation or fulfillment. It becomes an invitation into deeper presence. We begin to feel the subtle layers of contraction that dissolve when awareness is brought into the body. We notice how breath deepens when we stop trying to perform connection. We feel how the heart softens when we allow ourselves to be met without shaping the moment. The body becomes more transparent, less guarded, more fluid. Intimacy becomes an unfolding, not an act.

In this way, intimacy trains the nervous system to remain open in increasing levels of sensation. Whether the sensation is emotional, physical, energetic, or erotic, the practice is the same: stay present. Let the experience move. Do not contract against it. Do not chase it. Do not seek to control it. Allow the energy to reveal where you brace and where you open. Allow the moment to show where identity tightens and where it dissolves. Through repeated experiences of being held, touched, seen, and received without collapsing into old patterns, the nervous system begins to reorganize itself around safety rather than fear, openness rather than defence, coherence rather than fragmentation.

As this occurs, intimacy becomes less about two people interacting and more about awareness meeting awareness through the bodies involved. The encounter becomes a field rather than an exchange. There is a spaciousness in which both beings are liberated from the need to perform or protect. Sensation becomes a doorway into truth. Presence becomes the unspoken language between bodies. Openness becomes the natural state rather than the achievement.

Eventually, intimacy becomes inseparable from awakening itself. It becomes a living classroom where the body remembers how to trust, how to soften, how to receive, and how to let go of the instinct to guard against closeness. The ego's structures dissolve not through effort but through continual experiences of safety in openness. And in this dissolution, intimacy reveals what it was always pointing toward: that the boundaries we cling to are not the truth of who we are. They are simply the remnants of old survival patterns dissolving in the presence of awareness.

When intimacy is met this way, it becomes not just relationship but revelation. A practice in remembering that separation was never real. A somatic doorway into unity. A place where the body learns to rest in the same spaciousness that consciousness has always known. Intimacy becomes awakening in motion — two bodies, one field, dissolving into the simplicity of being.

Chapter 12

Merging, Surrender, Presence, and Embodied Union

Merging is not about losing oneself in another; it is about dissolving the contraction that once defined the edges of the self. It is the moment when the nervous system releases its grip on separation and allows two bodies, two fields, two expressions of consciousness to move as one current. True merging cannot be forced, performed, or manufactured. It arises only when both systems are relaxed enough, open enough, and coherent enough to let awareness flow without interruption. In this state, intimacy becomes less like an encounter and more like a shared awakening — an experience of unity that the body feels before the mind can name it.

Surrender is the threshold into this unity. It is not the submission of will or the abandonment of boundaries; it is the softening of protective structures that no longer serve the moment. Surrender is the body's way of saying, *There is nothing to defend here. The moment is safe enough for me to let life move through.* It is a yielding, not to another person, but to the deeper intelligence animating both people. The ego loosens. Identity softens. The need to manage, predict, or control dissolves. What remains is breath, sensation, aliveness — moving freely through a system that is no longer resisting itself.

Presence is the container that makes surrender possible. Without presence, the experience collapses into intensity, fantasy, or dissociation. With presence, the body becomes grounded enough to receive what is unfolding. Presence slows the moment, expands the space, and creates a field in which nothing needs to be rushed. In presence, even subtle gestures become profound. Touch carries awareness rather than agenda. Breathing becomes synchronicity rather than habit. Every sensation is allowed to rise and fall in its natural rhythm, without bracing or amplification. Presence makes intimacy less about doing and more about being.

When merging, surrender, and presence converge, embodied union becomes possible. This is not merely union of bodies but union of fields — an experience where two awarenesses recognize themselves as expressions of the same Source. Identity becomes translucent. The sense of “I” softens into “we,” and then dissolves into something even more spacious. The encounter shifts from personal to transpersonal, from relational to revelatory. There is a quiet recognition: *This is what my heart has always known. There is only one consciousness here, playing in two forms.*

In embodied union, sexual energy no longer moves in isolated loops. It circulates between and through both bodies as if guided by an unseen intelligence. Pleasure expands beyond localized sensation, radiating through the chest, the spine, the belly, the limbs — sometimes even beyond the physical form. The experience becomes energetic, emotional, and spacious all at once. The boundary between self and other becomes permeable, and what remains is a sense of being moved by something far greater than desire. The body becomes an instrument of awakening, and intimacy becomes a somatic experience of non-duality.

This depth of union does not occur because two people are compatible in personality or preference. It arises because both have softened enough to let awareness lead the moment. The merging is guided not by technique but by coherence. The surrender is supported not by trust in the other, but by trust in the intelligence moving through both. Presence anchors the experience so that the body can remain open to the truth it is remembering.

Embodied union is the lived dissolution of separation. It is the moment when form and formlessness touch, when two bodies reveal the oneness that has always existed beneath them. In this space, intimacy becomes a doorway into the deepest reality: that consciousness is not contained within individuals. It moves freely through all of us, and in moments of profound openness, it allows us to feel — viscerally, undeniably — that we were never separate to begin with.

Where the Body Remembers Unity

Sexuality and intimacy ultimately reveal what the mind cannot grasp: awakening is not an escape from the body, but a deep return into it. Every contraction around touch, pleasure, vulnerability, and closeness is a doorway into the places where separation still lives in our physiology. And every moment of openness — every breath that softens, every wave of sensation we allow, every instance we stay present in connection — becomes a step toward remembering who we are beneath the ego's architecture of survival.

In the end, sexuality is not about desire, performance, or identity. It is about the capacity of the body to receive life without resistance. Intimacy is not about finding the perfect partner or achieving the ideal experience. It is about meeting another human being without the distortions of fear, without the protections of conditioning, without the reflexive bracing that once defined our sense of self. These encounters show us what remains defended and what is ready to open. They show us where we are still holding onto an identity that no longer needs to be protected. They show us the difference between wanting connection and being available for it.

As the nervous system reorganizes around safety rather than survival, intimacy becomes a practice of presence, not performance. Sexual energy becomes an expression of Source, not tension. Merging becomes a remembering, not a losing. The body, once shaped by contraction, becomes available for the truth that has always lived beneath it: unity is not something to achieve; it is something we feel when we release the layers that once obscured it.

In this light, sexuality becomes sacred — not because of ritual or philosophy, but because of the depth of awareness that flows through it. The simplest touch becomes profound when the body is open. The quietest breath becomes revelatory when the heart is unguarded. Intimacy becomes a mirror in which we recognize the innocence beneath all our defences and the vastness beneath all our fears. Through this recognition, the illusion of separation begins to dissolve, not through force, but through presence.

What emerges is a new relationship with the body, with love, and with the divine intelligence moving through all things. We begin to experience intimacy not as a path toward another person, but as a path back into the deepest truth of ourselves. Sexuality becomes a doorway where the personal meets the infinite. Presence becomes the bridge. Union becomes the remembrance.

And in this remembrance, the body finally reveals what it has known all along: awakening is not somewhere we travel to. It is what arises when we stop resisting the places where life wants to enter us. It is the moment consciousness meets itself through form, through sensation, through connection — and recognizes, with humility and wonder, that there was never anything to protect, and never anything to separate from.

As we conclude this exploration, let it be clear that sexuality is not a requirement for awakening, nor is it a superior spiritual path. It is simply one of the places where the body reveals its truth most vividly. The contractions that arise in intimacy are not signs of inadequacy — they are signals of where the nervous system still seeks safety.

The openings that emerge are not achievements — they are reminders of the unity that has always lived beneath our defences. Sexuality becomes a doorway only because it brings us into direct contact with the fundamental movements of receiving, surrender, presence, and connection. Whether you walk this doorway or another, the essence remains the same: awakening is the softening of separation. And as you move into the next chapter, you will see that the heart of this entire path — whether in intimacy, in relationship, in abundance, or in daily life — is learning how to let life in.

V

Expansion, Receiving, and Creation

Chapter

13

The Somatic Path to Receiving

As we step from intimacy into receiving, it becomes clear that the same openings that allow us to let another human being in are the openings that allow life itself to reach us. What dissolves in union is the same contraction that prevents abundance, love, support, and possibility from landing in the body. In this way, receiving is not a different skill but a continuation of the same somatic softening — another doorway through which the nervous system learns to trust openness as its natural state.

Why Receiving Is a Nervous System Skill

Receiving is not a mindset, nor is it a technique one can perform through willpower. It is not an affirmation, a financial strategy, or a spiritual declaration. Receiving is a physiological capacity — a learned openness in the body that allows life to enter without triggering contraction, defence, or withdrawal. To receive is to remain undefended in the presence of goodness. And for most people, this is far more challenging than they consciously realize.

The nervous system is shaped by what it has known, not by what we desire. If the body has been trained to brace, to predict danger, to prepare for loss or disappointment, then even supportive experiences can feel overwhelming. Love can feel too intimate. Praise can feel exposing. Opportunities can feel threatening. Abundance can feel destabilizing. Not because the experience is unsafe — but because openness itself was never practiced, never reinforced, never allowed to become familiar.

This is why so many people say they want more — more love, more connection, more ease, more wealth — yet internally flinch the moment something real arrives. The body closes before the mind understands what happened. Receiving is not blocked at the level of belief; it is blocked at the level of sensation. The nervous system contracts to maintain what it knows, not because it is "self-sabotaging," but because it is loyal to the familiar rhythms of survival.

When receiving begins to deepen, it is not because one has forced themselves to "be more open." It is because the body starts to learn that openness does not equal threat — that softening does not mean danger, that allowing does not mean losing control. This shift happens slowly, as awareness meets the subtle micro-flinches, the background tension, the invisible bracing that once defined our relationship with life. As presence begins to hold these patterns instead of resisting them, the nervous system discovers that it can expand, breathe, and let experience in without collapsing.

Receiving, then, becomes a somatic unfolding — a reorganization of the body around safety, not survival. It is the nervous system's gradual recognition that life is not an adversary to defend against, but a movement of support continually flowing toward us. As this recognition stabilizes, capacity grows. What once felt overwhelming becomes natural. What once threatened identity now nourishes it. What once triggered retreat now evokes gratitude.

In this way, receiving becomes less about acquiring and more about allowing. Less about grasping and more about opening. It becomes the embodied expression of unity — the moment when the boundary between "me" and "life" softens, and the body learns it is safe to be met, filled, touched, supported. To receive is to remember that we are not separate from what we long for. It is the nervous system, finally relaxing into its original truth: openness is our natural state, and life is always trying to enter us the moment we have the capacity to let it.

Contraction Around Love, Money, Praise, Intimacy

Contraction is the nervous system's first language. It is the body's ancient way of saying, *This is too much,* even when what is arriving is exactly what we've longed for. Most people believe they contract around danger or discomfort, but in truth, we contract most deeply around the experiences that touch our core — love, abundance, appreciation, and intimacy. These are not merely external events; they are openings. They require us to be seen, to be receptive, to allow ourselves to be affected. And for a nervous system conditioned to survive through self-protection, openness can feel like the greatest risk of all.

When love approaches — sincere, present, steady — many feel an inexplicable tightening in the chest, a holding in the breath, a retreat inward. Love exposes the places within us that still believe we are unworthy, unlovable, or unsafe to depend on another. The contraction is not resistance to love itself, but resistance to being touched at the level where identity once formed around lack or abandonment. The body shields itself not because love is dangerous, but because receiving love would require the dissolution of old stories the nervous system still holds as truth.

Money evokes a similar pattern. Abundance brings expansion, and expansion threatens the familiarity of limitation. Even when we intellectually desire prosperity, the body often tightens in response to it. Sudden opportunities, unexpected financial success, or even the idea of having enough can trigger the contraction of "too much," as if the body fears it cannot hold what is arriving. For many, wealth challenges a survival identity built around striving, scarcity, or vigilance. The nervous system does not contract around money — it contracts around the unfamiliar spaciousness that money represents.

Praise touches another vulnerable layer. To be acknowledged, seen, or valued can feel disorienting when the body has learned to stay small to stay safe. Appreciation lands directly on the places where shame or inadequacy once rooted themselves. Praise threatens the protective structures of self-criticism and invisibility, so the nervous system contracts to maintain an identity that has been built out of old wounds. Compliments then become uncomfortable not because we don't want them, but because they shine light into the very places we once hid.

And intimacy — the space where two nervous systems meet without armour — reveals the deepest contraction of all. True intimacy is not merely physical; it is the dissolving of the emotional and energetic distance we've used to feel stable. When someone gets close enough to touch the raw, unguarded parts of our humanity, the body may brace instinctively. Opening in intimacy requires a surrender that survival physiology was never designed to permit. The contraction is not a rejection of the other person; it is a final attempt to protect the remnants of separation.

Each of these contractions — around love, money, praise, and intimacy — arises from the same root: the body's loyalty to the familiar, even when the familiar is painful. Receiving is threatening only to the identity that was built in its absence. But as awareness meets these contractions with compassion rather than judgment, the nervous system begins to learn a new truth: that what once overwhelmed us is now safe, that openness will not destroy us, and that we are capable of holding more than we ever believed.

This is the somatic path of receiving — the gradual unwinding of the old survival structures that once closed us to life, so we can finally let in what has always been trying to reach us.

Expanding Capacity Through Safety and Presence

Capacity does not expand through force. It does not stretch because we demand it to, or because we intellectually understand that we "should be able" to receive more. Capacity expands the same way the body unwinds after years of bracing: through safety, through presence, through a slow and organic reorganization of the nervous system. What we call "receiving more" is, at its core, the body remembering that openness is not a threat.

Safety is not an idea — it is a physiological experience. The body knows when it is being pushed, when it is being rushed, when it is being asked to hold more than it can genuinely integrate. And the moment the body senses overwhelm, it contracts. This is why receiving cannot be forced, and why affirmations or "just be open" rarely touch the deeper layers. The nervous system responds not to intention, but to felt regulation.

If the inner environment is tense, guarded, or vigilant, no amount of wanting can override the body's instinctive retreat.

But presence changes everything. Presence is the field that tells the body, *You are not alone in this experience.* Presence is the awareness that meets sensation without pressure, without agenda, without the unconscious demand to "get over this contraction." When presence is stable, the nervous system feels held. And when it feels held, it begins to soften. In this softness, the edges of our capacity naturally expand — not because we stretch them, but because the body feels safe enough to allow more life in.

This is why so much of receiving is really about learning to stay with ourselves in the moments when we would normally abandon, override, or tighten. The trembling in the chest when someone expresses genuine care. The fluttering in the belly when abundance approaches. The heat in the body when praise lands. The vulnerability that shows up when intimacy draws near. These sensations are not signs that we are incapable — they are invitations for presence. To sit with the intensity, not to collapse into it, and not to run from it, but to meet it with the same gentle witnessing that dissolves all other contractions.

As presence deepens, the nervous system begins to interpret openness differently. What once felt overwhelming becomes manageable. What once triggered a shutdown becomes a doorway. What once felt unsafe becomes familiar. Capacity does not expand in dramatic leaps, but in quiet increments — the breath that drops a little lower, the chest that softens a little more, the heart that remains open for an extra second before bracing. Over time, these seconds accumulate into a new baseline.

This is the somatic path: expanding capacity not by stretching into more, but by resting deeply into what is here. When the body learns that no sensation is too much for our awareness to hold, receiving becomes natural. Safety and presence rewire the nervous system to trust openness again. And in this trust, life can finally enter us without resistance — not as something we try to manage, but as something we now have the capacity to welcome.

Repatterning Receiving Through Awareness

Repatterning receiving is not a matter of convincing the mind that we deserve more. It is the quiet, steady re-education of the body — a shift in how sensation is interpreted, how openness is experienced, and how life is allowed to touch us. Awareness is the intelligence that makes this repatterning possible. Not mental analysis, not self-improvement strategies, but the simple, direct presence that sees the body's contraction with compassion instead of urgency.

Every old pattern of non-receiving is rooted in a moment where the nervous system learned that opening was not safe. The child who reached for love and found inconsistency learned to close. The young adult who stepped toward opportunity and met failure learned to brace. The person who felt seen and then shamed learned to disappear. These imprints do not unwind through positive thinking; they unwind when awareness meets the exact felt sense that once overwhelmed us, but this time without abandoning the body.

Awareness rewires the nervous system by becoming the stable reference point that the body never had. When contraction arises — the tightening in the solar plexus, the lift in the shoulders, the shallowing of breath — awareness does not try to fix it. It observes it. It softens around it. It allows the sensation to unfold in its own timing. Over and over, the body receives the message: *This experience is allowed. This intensity is safe. Nothing needs to be pushed away.*

In this space, new patterns emerge naturally. The body begins to associate openness not with danger, but with presence. Receiving becomes less like stepping into the unknown and more like returning to something familiar. As awareness stays with each micro-contraction, the pattern reorganizes: the heart opens a fraction more before bracing; the breath flows a little deeper before tightening; the body begins to trust that what is arriving is not too much to hold.

Repatterning is not dramatic. It is subtle. It is the dissolving of the reflex to shrink, the softening of the impulse to protect, the gradual release of the belief that we must manage life alone. Awareness replaces past conditioning with new lived evidence: *I can remain open. I can let this in. I can feel this and still be safe.* And as this becomes the body's new truth, the old survival strategies lose their grip.

In time, receiving becomes effortless — not because the circumstances have changed, but because the inner environment has. Awareness has rewoven the somatic patterns that once rejected abundance, intimacy, praise, or love. The nervous system now recognizes openness as the natural state. Receiving becomes the organic extension of being present, the way a flower opens not through effort but through alignment with its nature.

This is how awareness repatterns receiving: not by pushing the body toward expansion, but by holding it so faithfully that expansion becomes inevitable.

Receiving as the Embodiment of Unity

Receiving is not merely an emotional openness or a psychological shift — it is the lived expression of non-duality within the body. When the nervous system softens enough to let life in, we are not just accepting love, abundance, praise, or intimacy; we are dissolving the illusion that we are separate from the very forces that nourish us. Receiving is unity made tangible. It is the moment the body remembers that it is not an isolated self defending against existence, but a porous, interconnected expression of the same intelligence that gives rise to every experience.

In this way, receiving is one of the most direct somatic gateways into oneness. The contraction that once kept life at a distance is the physical form of separation. It is the body insisting on "me versus life," "me versus the world," "me versus the unknown." When we receive, that barrier softens. The boundary between giver and receiver becomes less rigid. The fear-based internal posture of *I must protect myself* is replaced with the felt sense of *life is meeting me, and I can allow it.*The nervous system shifts from defence into communion.

At higher states of awareness, receiving is no longer something you "do." It becomes a natural symmetry between the inner and outer fields — a reciprocal flow where what enters you is not perceived as coming from outside, but as arising within the same unified field of consciousness. Love does not arrive from another person; it emerges within the space of connection that includes both of you. Praise does not come from an external source validating your worth; it surfaces from the recognition that awareness is expressing itself through form. Opportunities do not come “to you”; they unfold as extensions of your own coherence.

This is why receiving is so fundamentally spiritual. It is not about acquiring anything. It is about dissolving the internal divisions that once made receiving impossible. When the body rests in openness, unity is no longer a concept — it is a lived, felt, undeniable truth. The breath deepens, the heart expands, the subtle field around the body grows more permeable, and life feels less like something happening around you and more like something flowing through you.

And there is a quiet miracle in this: the more you are able to receive, the more you realize that giving and receiving are the same movement. The same openness that allows love in allows love out. The same nervous system that can hold abundance can also express generosity. The same heart that can soften in intimacy becomes the heart that offers presence effortlessly. Receiving is not a passive state; it is the recognition that life circulates through you when you stop interrupting the flow.

To embody receiving is to embody unity. It is to live without the hardened edges that once defined the ego’s existence. It is to allow the world, other beings, and the intelligence of life to touch you deeply — without fear, without contraction, without retreat. When the nervous system learns to stay open in this way, you become a conduit for the movement of Source. Not separate from it, not reaching for it, but expressing it. And in that expression, receiving becomes the most natural, effortless, and sacred act of remembering who you truly are.

Chapter 13

The Return to Open Hands

Receiving is not a lesson the mind masters; it is a remembrance the body reclaims. Throughout this chapter, what becomes clear is that receiving is not about accumulating more, performing worthiness, or forcing ourselves to be open. It is the steady, compassionate unwinding of the survival patterns that once taught us that openness was dangerous and that life had to be managed rather than allowed.

The path to receiving is ultimately the path back to ourselves — back to the unguarded state where life can meet us without armour, without performance, without contraction. As awareness begins to hold the old reflexes with tenderness, the body learns to trust what it once feared. It discovers that love does not overwhelm, that abundance does not destabilize, that praise does not threaten identity, and that intimacy does not require losing oneself.

Receiving becomes the natural expression of a system no longer bracing against life. It is the embodied recognition that separation was never our truth. As the nervous system relaxes, unity becomes more than a spiritual idea — it becomes the felt experience of being in relationship with all things.

To receive fully is to live with open hands: not grasping, not controlling, not defending. Open hands symbolize a body that trusts, a heart that softens, and an awareness that recognizes everything arriving in our lives as part of the same field of intelligence we arise from. When the body stops tightening against experience, receiving is as natural as breathing, as effortless as presence, as fluid as the unfolding of consciousness itself.

And so the somatic path to receiving is, in the end, the path of remembering who we are beneath all the tension we once carried. It is the quiet return to openness, where life can flow freely again — through us, into us, and as us.

Chapter

14

The Somatic Basis of Abundance and Manifestation

Creation Through Coherence, Not Force

Creation, at its deepest level, is not something the separate self does. It is what arises when the body is no longer braced against life. When the nervous system softens out of survival and returns to its natural coherence, manifestation becomes less an act of will and more a natural unfolding — like breath, like the tides, like the quiet intelligence that grows a tree without strain. In coherence, creation is not pushed; it is permitted.

Force belongs to the realm of separation. It is the strategy of a body that does not yet believe it is safe to open, safe to receive, or safe to be guided by something deeper than thought. When the nervous system holds contraction, the ego tries to make life happen through pressure, discipline, and mental dominance. It tries to think its way toward abundance while the body is still patterned around lack. But creation cannot emerge cleanly from a physiology shaped by fear. The signal is distorted before it ever reaches the world.

Coherence, on the other hand, is the somatic signature of alignment. It is felt as an inner synchronization — the heart restful, the breath unforced, the mind quiet enough for deeper intelligence to surface. When the body settles, clarity returns.

When clarity returns, intention becomes simple, clean, and undivided. This is why the deepest creations do not feel like effort: they feel like inevitability. They arise from the same field that moves galaxies and opens flowers, the same unity that pulses beneath thought and identity.

You have experienced this in your own life: the moments when everything feels effortless, when the next step appears without pressure, when synchronicity replaces struggle. These are not accidents. They are reflections of the state you are in. Coherence organizes reality around it. Just as a regulated body brings safety to a room, a coherent being brings order to circumstances, opportunities, and outcomes. Not by imposing, but by resonating.

In this way, manifestation becomes less a technique and more a frequency. Abundance is not summoned through desire or intensity; it is allowed through openness. The more the body relaxes out of survival, the more easily life can flow through it. What you create is no longer the expression of your fear or striving — it is the expression of your inner unity. It is creation that emerges because you are clear, not because you are trying to be.

Coherence is the end of effort as identity. It is the remembering that life itself is the creator, and that your body — when unguarded and aligned — is its perfect instrument.

Why the Ego Struggles to Manifest Cleanly

The ego cannot manifest cleanly because it does not create from wholeness — it creates from incompleteness. Every intention formed inside the egoic structure is shaped by contraction, fear, and survival. It is not that the ego is wrong; it is simply limited. It tries to manifest abundance while living in a body still patterned around lack. It tries to create expansion while holding itself tight. And so its creations arrive distorted, conflicted, or unsustainable, because they are born from a physiology that is braced against life.

The ego's desires are not pure desires — they are compensations. They come from the belief that something is missing, and that external acquisition will fill the gap. But the gap is not in the world; it is in the nervous system. When the body is carrying unprocessed fear, shame, or unworthiness, the ego will try to manifest from these states — seeking validation, safety, or significance through outcomes. What it creates is never clean because the intention behind it is never free. The signal is cluttered before it ever reaches the field of possibility.

This is why ego-driven manifestation often feels like effort, pushing, grasping, or chasing. The ego does not know how to trust. It only knows how to control. And control is incompatible with true creation. Control narrows the universe to what the mind can understand, while clean manifestation arises from the deeper intelligence beneath thought. The ego wants guarantees. Life offers emergence. The two do not meet until the body softens enough for trust to return.

The ego struggles because it is fundamentally future-oriented. It manifests from "When I get there, I'll finally be okay." But creation happens only from presence. Presence requires a regulated body. When the nervous system is dysregulated, the ego pulls the mind into timelines of danger, urgency, or deficiency. It tries to manifest from a state that says, "I'm not safe yet." And what you manifest from is what you amplify. If the underlying state is fear, the creation reinforces fear. If the underlying state is lack, the manifestation strengthens lack.

Clean manifestation does not arise from the ego because the ego's job is not to create — it is to protect. And when protection runs the system, creation becomes secondary to survival. The mind may visualize abundance, but the body is still preparing for loss. The mind may set goals for expansion, but the physiology is still braced for threat. These conflicting signals cancel each other out, making manifestation feel blocked, delayed, or chaotic.

When the ego relaxes, when the body softens out of its survival patterns, when awareness reclaims the space that fear once occupied — only then does creation become clean. Not because the technique changes, but because the one who is creating has. Creation becomes the natural expression of coherence, rather than the desperate attempt of a fractured self trying to secure its existence. In this way, manifestation becomes not a strategy, but a reflection of your inner state.

Nervous System Capacity as the Limit of Abundance

Abundance is not limited by desire, vision, talent, or even opportunity. It is limited by the capacity of the nervous system to hold expansion without collapsing back into old patterns of fear and contraction. Every level of abundance — whether financial, relational, emotional, or spiritual — requires a corresponding level of somatic openness. Without this openness, the body interprets expansion as danger, and what the ego calls "self-sabotage" is simply the nervous system protecting itself from overwhelm.

The body is always honest. It will only allow you to experience the amount of abundance it feels safe to receive. When the system is unconsciously braced, abundance feels like too much. Too much attention, too much love, too much responsibility, too much visibility, too much change. The mind may say, "I want more," but the body says, "More threatens the familiar pattern." And the body wins every time. Not because it is flawed, but because it is wired for survival, not prosperity.

This is why people often manifest small improvements but struggle with larger shifts. The nervous system can tolerate minor expansions, but when life begins to open in a way that challenges the old identity, it pulls back. A larger income collapses into unexpected bills. A deepening relationship triggers distancing. A breakthrough opportunity is met with hesitation or confusion. These are not failures — they are expressions of capacity. The system contracts to return to what it knows, even if what it knows is limitation.

Your abundance is never blocked; it is regulated. It matches the bandwidth your body has for openness, uncertainty, and receiving. When the nervous system is spacious, grounded, and coherent, abundance becomes natural because the body does not resist it. But when the system is dysregulated, abundance becomes destabilizing. The body shuts down opportunities it cannot metabolize.

In this way, abundance becomes a somatic practice. You do not expand your life by forcing larger outcomes — you expand your life by expanding your capacity to feel, to stay present, to remain open in the face of possibility. As the system learns safety through awareness, breath, presence, and connection to Source, it gradually widens its window of tolerance. You become able to hold more life without collapsing, bracing, or withdrawing. And the moment you can hold more, more arrives.

The truth is simple: abundance does not transform you; you transform into the one who can hold abundance. The outer world rearranges around the inner coherence you embody. When the nervous system opens, life expands to meet it.

Embodied Alignment With Source

Alignment with Source is not a philosophical position or a spiritual concept — it is a somatic reality. It is felt in the body long before it is understood in the mind. When the nervous system is regulated, open, and coherent, the body becomes permeable to a deeper intelligence that moves through it with effortless clarity. What you call intuition, guidance, or inner knowing is simply the absence of interference. It is the experience of Source moving unobstructed through form.

Embodied alignment arises when you stop bracing against life. The contraction of the ego — its fear, its vigilance, its need for control — creates static in the system. This static distorts the natural flow of truth, making your own inner signals harder to feel. But as the body softens, as survival loosens its grip, you begin to sense a subtler rhythm beneath the noise. You begin to feel that your life has a current, and that this current is not random, but intelligent. You align with Source not by striving upward, but by relaxing inward.

In this state, discernment becomes effortless. You do not analyze possibilities — you feel resonance. You do not chase outcomes — you follow the deeper movement that is already unfolding. Alignment is never about making decisions with greater force; it is about allowing decisions to arise from a quieter, deeper place within you. When the nervous system is grounded, the field of awareness becomes unobstructed, and guidance emerges with a simplicity the ego could never fabricate.

This alignment is not passive. It is profoundly active, but not in the way the ego understands activity. It is activity guided by coherence, not urgency; action initiated by clarity, not fear. You move not because you are escaping something behind you, but because you are answering something ahead of you. In embodied alignment, your actions do not feel like choices — they feel like the natural expression of who you already are.

The more the body remembers its safety, the more you feel inseparable from the intelligence that animates all things. This dissolves the illusion that you are the one "manifesting" anything. Instead, creation becomes a collaborative movement: Source expressing through your form, your form responding to Source. You become both the vessel and the expression. The boundary between personal desire and universal intention begins to blur, until what you want and what life wants through you are the same.

This is the true foundation of abundance. Not effort. Not visualization. Not strategic manifestation. But the somatic recognition that you are already in relationship with the creative force of existence. When you align with it — when your body becomes an open channel rather than a defended structure — life flows through you with a grace that feels almost inevitable. You do not create abundance; you allow abundance to express itself through your embodied connection to Source.

Manifestation as the Flow of Unity Through Form

Manifestation, in its purest essence, is not about acquiring outcomes — it is about allowing the movement of unity to become visible through your life. It is the process by which the undivided field of awareness expresses itself as form, guided not by personal will but by the deeper intelligence that animates everything. When the body is open and coherent, you become a conduit for this movement. When the body is contracted, the flow distorts, fragments, or halts. Abundance is simply the natural consequence of becoming permeable to the unity that is always trying to express through you.

In unity, there is no separation between inner intention and outer experience. What arises within you is already connected to the larger field that responds to it. But for most people, the nervous system interrupts this connection. Old survival patterns create static, blocking the felt sense of unity and replacing it with fear-driven strategies. Manifestation then becomes a struggle because the ego tries to create without access to the deeper current it is meant to ride. It forces what is meant to flow.

But as the system softens, something remarkable begins to happen: you feel the world from the inside. You sense the subtle continuity between your inner state and the movements of life around you. You begin to recognize that your intentions are not isolated impulses but waves originating from the same ocean that shapes circumstances, relationships, timing, and opportunity. Manifestation becomes the natural alignment between your inner state and the field that holds all possibilities. When unity flows unobstructed through form, life organizes itself with an elegance that feels like synchronicity, but is actually coherence.

This flow expresses itself not through pushing but through attunement. You feel when to move, when to wait, when to speak, when to rest. You stop trying to bend the world toward your desires and instead let your desires emerge from the same intelligence that orchestrates your path. In this way, manifestation becomes less about “making things happen” and more about participating in the unfolding that is already happening. The less you resist, the clearer the flow becomes.

When unity moves through a regulated, open body, your creations carry its signature: ease, clarity, naturalness, inevitability. They do not feel like the products of effort but like the next expression of who you are becoming. They arise from the same stillness that underlies all of existence. The world responds not to your force, but to your frequency — because the frequency you hold is the imprint of the unity you embody.

In this sense, manifestation is never something added to you; it is something revealed through you. It is unity translating itself into form through the channel of your body, your presence, your coherence. And as you continue to dissolve the remnants of separation, the flow becomes ever more direct. Manifestation becomes not a practice, but a way of being. Life expresses through you, as you, in an unbroken continuity of abundance and awareness.

The Body as the Doorway to Living Creation

Abundance is not achieved; it is remembered. It is not the result of effort, intention, or spiritual technique, but the natural expression of a body that is no longer braced against life. When the nervous system settles out of survival and returns to its innate coherence, you rediscover that creation is not something you do — it is something you are continuously participating in. Manifestation becomes the movement of unity through your form, an effortless unfolding guided by the deeper intelligence that animates existence itself.

Everything in this chapter points to a single truth: the body is the gateway. Your capacity to receive, to expand, to act, to trust, to be guided, and to allow abundance is determined not by your mind's beliefs but by your physiology's openness. The ego will always try to manifest through force because it was born in contraction. But awareness, grounded in the body, reveals a new way of creating — one where life is no longer pushed, managed, or chased, but flowed with.

As you soften into this truth, you begin to see the world differently. Opportunities no longer feel separate from you; they feel like extensions of your inner coherence. Guidance becomes clear, not because you think more clearly, but because you no longer interfere with the deeper current moving through you. Abundance stops feeling like an external achievement and becomes a reflection of your somatic state — an echo of your inner alignment with Source.

In the end, manifestation is not about becoming powerful; it is about becoming permeable. It is about letting the unity beneath all things express itself through your particular form. When the body is open, life moves through you with precision. When the body is coherent, creation becomes natural. And when the body remembers its inherent safety, abundance is not something you pursue — it is the environment you inhabit.

This is the somatic basis of true manifestation: not the acquisition of more, but the dissolution of everything that constricts the flow of what already wants to move through you.

Chapter

15

Living Without Bracing: The End of Survival

Life Without Contraction

To imagine a life without contraction is to imagine a life where the body is no longer quietly preparing for impact. It is the end of the subtle flinching that has shaped one's entire way of being. Most people never notice how much of their identity is built around bracing — how the shoulders lift a few millimetres in anticipation of pressure, how the breath hides in the upper chest, how the belly stiffens just enough to feel in control. Contraction becomes so familiar that openness feels almost foreign, like a country glimpsed in dreams but never inhabited. And yet, the truth is that the body was never designed to live in contraction. It only learned to because it once had to.

A life without contraction is not a life free of sensation, experience, or challenge. It is a life where none of these require the body to shrink around them. It is the recognition that the world does not need to be managed from tension. When contraction dissolves, experience is no longer something to brace for but something to meet. The body shifts from anticipating threat to receiving life. This shift is subtle, but it transforms everything. Instead of tightening when uncertainty arises, the body softens. Instead of preparing for a blow that never comes, it relaxes into presence. Instead of controlling reality, it allows reality to unfold.

In this openness, life stops feeling like a sequence of obstacles to navigate and becomes a continuous movement of expression. You begin to notice the natural intelligence inside your tissues — the way breath flows without instruction, the way intuition moves before thought, the way clarity arises when there is nothing to protect. Without contraction, the nervous system no longer filters the world through danger; it perceives directly. Sensation loses its charge and becomes simply sensation. Emotion no longer threatens identity because identity is no longer built on tension. Even the mind quiets, not because you forced it to, but because there is nothing left to defend.

To live without contraction is to rediscover how vast you actually are. Survival shrinks your sense of self; openness restores it. What emerges is a state of unguardedness that is not naïve but deeply intelligent — a trust that comes not from belief but from the body's lived experience of safety. In this state, life meets you differently. Relationships soften. Opportunities expand. The world seems more resonant, not because it changed, but because you are no longer approaching it from a clenched posture. You are no longer the one who braces. You are the one who receives.

This is the beginning of living beyond survival. Not an idea, not a philosophy, but a somatic reality: a body that no longer flinches at life. A body that remembers openness as its natural state. A life that unfolds from the absence of contraction, where clarity is not sought but revealed, and where freedom is not something attained but something finally permitted to be felt.

Chapter 15

Trust as a Somatic State

Trust is often spoken about as if it were a belief, a mindset, or a decision one makes with the mind. But trust cannot be manufactured through thought. You can repeat the words "I trust" a thousand times, and still feel the body contract at the slightest hint of uncertainty. True trust is not an affirmation — it is a physiological state. It is the body's willingness to remain open in the presence of the unknown. It is the nervous system resting in safety even when the future cannot be predicted. Trust begins where the mind's control ends.

When the body is shaped by survival, trust is impossible. The nervous system is trained to scan for danger, anticipate loss, and brace for disappointment. In this state, even positive experiences feel unstable, as though they could vanish at any moment. This is why trust is not restored by convincing yourself the world is safe; it is restored when the body experiences itself as safe. Only then does the protective vigilance soften. Only then does the breath drop lower into the belly. Only then does the heart open without feeling exposed. Trust is the natural consequence of a system no longer preparing for harm.

To feel trust somatically is to feel the body settle into a deeper rhythm. There is a quieting that happens — not the quiet of dissociation, but the quiet of alignment. You sense that you are supported from within, held by something greater than your strategies. The ground beneath your life becomes less rigid, yet more stable. You no longer need to predict the future to feel secure because your security is not dependent on outcomes — it arises from presence. Trust becomes the felt knowing that life moves with you, not against you.

As trust deepens, the body stops insisting on tension as a form of preparedness. Your chest loosens. Your jaw softens. The micro-flinches dissolve. You begin to move through the world with an internal ease that does not ask for guarantees. This is the shift from survival to openness: your system no longer interprets the unknown as a threat. The unknown becomes spacious, inviting, even creative. You start to meet life with curiosity instead of caution. And in this openness, opportunities that once felt too risky now feel natural and aligned.

A somatically trusting body is not naïve; it is wise. It has learned that contraction was never safety — it was only habit. It has learned that the deepest form of protection is coherence, not tension. It has learned that presence itself is intelligence. When trust is lived in the body, you no longer have to force yourself to let go. Letting go becomes the organic response of a system that finally recognizes it is held. This is the essence of embodied trust: not something you declare, but something you become.

Moving Through the World from Openness

To move through the world from openness is to inhabit a fundamentally different orientation to life. Most people navigate their days through subtle defence — planning, predicting, managing, tightening around what might go wrong. Even when nothing overtly threatening is happening, the body carries a quiet readiness to contract. Openness, by contrast, is not a strategy but a state of being. It is the body's natural expression when it no longer anticipates harm. It is the unguarded way of moving that arises when survival is no longer the lens through which reality is interpreted.

When you move from openness, you enter each moment without bracing for the next. There is no pre-emptive tension shaping your choices, no inner argument with the unfolding of life. Instead, there is a relaxed responsiveness. You meet situations directly, without filtering them through old fear patterns. The body remains soft even when facing challenge — not because challenge disappears, but because you no longer collapse into the belief that danger lives everywhere. Openness gives you access to clarity that contraction could never provide. In this state, intuition becomes more accurate, decisions become more fluid, and your movements become more aligned.

Openness does not mean vulnerability in the old sense of being unprotected; it means your protection is no longer based on closing. The nervous system stops interpreting presence as exposure. Your boundaries become clearer, not harsher, because they arise from awareness rather than fear. You say no without bracing. You say yes without grasping. You move through relationships with a steadiness that comes from inner coherence rather than outer control. People feel safer around you because your energy is not charged with defence. You participate in life without the armour that once distorted your perception.

From openness, action becomes effortless. You no longer push yourself forward through force, nor do you shrink backward in hesitation. Instead, you follow the natural flow of inner signals — your body's subtle movements, the shifts in your emotional field, the quiet intelligence that emerges when nothing is being resisted. Life becomes cooperative rather than adversarial. You do not need to create momentum; you attune to the momentum already moving through you. This is the grace that appears when contraction dissolves.

Ultimately, moving through the world from openness is the lived experience of freedom. It is the recognition that nothing needs to be tensed against, that presence itself is your stability. You are not navigating life from an armoured nervous system but from a relaxed, receptive one. And in that openness, you begin to experience the truth that has always been waiting beneath the bracing: life is not something you must resist — it is something you are meant to meet, to feel, to allow, and to move with as you remember your natural state.

The Body as an Instrument of Clarity

As contraction dissolves and the nervous system exits the survival posture, the body reveals a capacity that was always present but rarely accessible: it becomes an instrument of clarity. Most people try to think their way into understanding, forcing insight through mental effort. But the mind, when untethered from the body, becomes noisy, reactive, and easily distorted by old fear patterns. True clarity does not emerge from intellectual strain — it arises from a body that is no longer braced. When the system relaxes, perception sharpens. When tension quiets, truth becomes obvious.

A regulated, open body does not confuse preference with intuition or fear with guidance. It does not distort reality through the filters of old wounds. Instead, it responds to life with the precision of a tuning fork. Subtle signals — an expansion in the chest, a settling in the belly, a softening behind the sternum — become unmistakable indicators of alignment. Likewise, contraction, tightness, and agitation become clear signals of misalignment. You begin to realize that clarity has always been somatic. It is the body speaking before the mind interprets.

In this state, the body no longer operates as a repository for unresolved emotion or an archive of past danger; it becomes a living instrument, constantly attuning to what is true in the moment. Your internal movements become reliable. Your sensations become informative rather than overwhelming. You stop second-guessing yourself because your system is no longer echoing old survival patterns. Clarity becomes less about choosing correctly and more about feeling what is coherent. The body's neutrality reveals what the mind once complicated.

When you experience clarity somatically, decisions no longer require debate. You sense the path that carries resonance. You feel the opportunities that belong to you. You recognize the relationships that support your expansion. You know, without needing guarantees, which direction honours your integrity. This is clarity as embodiment — not an idea, but a direct perception arising from the absence of bracing. And because the body is free of the noise of fear, what remains is unmistakably simple.

As the body becomes an instrument of clarity, your life begins to reflect this inner coherence. Actions align. Words match inner truth. Movement follows intelligence rather than habit. You live less from reactivity and more from attunement. This is how awakening becomes practical: the body becomes the medium through which truth is felt, understood, and expressed. In this way, openness is not just a spiritual ideal but a functional, lived intelligence. With no contraction distorting the signal, the body becomes what it was always meant to be — a clear, resonant vessel through which awareness can guide your life.

Freedom as the Nervous System's Natural State

Freedom is not something you achieve at the end of healing, awakening, or personal development. It is not a prize earned through effort or discipline. Freedom is the nervous system's original, unconditioned state — the state it returns to the moment survival no longer dictates its posture. When the bracing softens and the vigilance dissolves, the system does not become empty or inert; it becomes spacious, fluid, and profoundly alive. Freedom is what emerges when the body is no longer organized around protection.

Most people assume freedom is the absence of limitation, but in truth, freedom is the absence of contraction. Contraction narrows perception, restricts movement, and shapes identity into something small and defensive. When the nervous system lives in survival, freedom feels impossible because the body is busy managing imagined threats. The world becomes tight around you, options shrink, possibilities feel dangerous, and even joy carries tension. But when the body releases the need to brace, freedom rises from within — effortlessly, naturally, unmistakably.

A free nervous system is not one without sensation; it is one that can feel everything without becoming overwhelmed. Emotions arise, move, and dissolve without defining you. Sensations flow through rather than locking into patterns of fear. The system becomes permeable, dynamic, and responsive. You experience life not as something to control, but as something to participate in. This is the nervous system's wisdom: freedom is not the absence of life's movements but the capacity to remain open through them.

In this state, choice becomes expansive. Not because you have more options, but because you are no longer constrained by the inner walls you once lived inside. Creativity returns. Vitality returns. Curiosity returns. You meet the unknown not with tension but with readiness. You discover a natural courage — not the forced kind that pushes through fear, but the quiet courage that appears when fear no longer governs your body. This is the freedom that emerges from coherence.

Freedom also carries a profound gentleness. There is no urgency, no desperation, no inner battle to win. The nervous system, once trapped in cycles of contraction, begins to express its true nature: openness, fluidity, and a grounded sense of being held. You feel life moving through you rather than pressing against you. You trust your experience. You trust your body. You trust existence.

This is the natural state of a system no longer shaped by survival — a state where freedom is not something you strive for, but something you finally remember.

The Softness That Remains

When the body no longer lives in a posture of defence, something profoundly simple reveals itself — something so natural it is easy to overlook, yet so transformative it reshapes the entire experience of being human. What remains after the dissolution of bracing is not a grand spiritual state or a dramatic inner breakthrough. It is softness. A quiet, effortless softness that permeates breath, movement, perception, and presence.

This softness is not weakness; it is the opposite. It is the strength that comes from no longer needing to protect what was never in danger. It is the resilience that arises when the nervous system is not compressing around imagined threats. It is the intelligence that emerges when openness becomes the default orientation. From this softness, the world feels different — not because the world changed, but because the lens of survival has finally fallen away.

Living without bracing is not a technique to master or a discipline to maintain. It is a return to the body's natural state — trustful, receptive, unguarded, attuned. It is the recognition that survival was once necessary, but it is no longer your home. As contraction fades, life ceases to be something that must be managed and becomes something that can be met. The nervous system, once shaped by fear, begins to express its true design: to move fluidly, feel fully, and participate freely.

This chapter marks the end of survival as an identity and the beginning of living as presence. When the body relaxes out of its lifelong anticipation of harm, clarity arises without searching, trust emerges without forcing, and freedom unfolds without striving. You discover that nothing was missing — only obscured by tension. The essence of who you are has always been spacious.

In the end, the journey of living without bracing is not a journey toward something new, but a journey back to what you already are. A body at ease. A heart unshielded. A life no longer contracted around fear. The softness that remains is the softness of your true nature — an openness that does not need to defend itself, because it is rooted in the unshakeable truth of your being.

VI

Embodied Awakening

Chapter

16

The Awakened Nervous System

Stability, Coherence, Depth

Stability in an awakened nervous system is not stiffness or stillness — it is the natural groundedness that emerges when nothing inside is being pushed, denied, or held apart. It is the steadiness that returns when the body no longer organizes itself around survival. Instead of bracing against life, the system settles into life. Instead of tightening around experience, it opens to experience. What remains is a stability that does not come from controlling the world, but from no longer needing to protect yourself from it.

This stability gives rise to coherence. Coherence is the internal alignment of sensation, emotion, thought, and presence — a unified movement rather than competing impulses fighting for dominance. In the unawakened state, the nervous system is fragmented: one part contracts, another part resists the contraction, another tries to override it with belief or intention. Awakening dissolves this fragmentation. The body becomes a single field, a harmonized expression rather than a divided one. Energy flows without interruption. Awareness moves through sensation without distortion. What you feel, what you know, and how you act come into integrity.

Depth emerges as the natural consequence of this coherence. When the body no longer reacts, the surface noise that once defined experience falls away. You begin to feel beneath the habitual layers of tension and narrative. Sensations become more textured, emotions more spacious, awareness more intimate. Depth is not something you seek; it is something that reveals itself when you are no longer collapsing into survival patterns. It is the quiet recognition that consciousness is not floating above the body but saturating it — permeating every cell, every breath, every pulse of aliveness.

Stability, coherence, and depth form the somatic foundation of awakened living. They do not come from effort, nor from spiritual ambition, but from the body's return to its natural, uncontracted state. When the nervous system is no longer shaped by fear, it naturally expresses truth. When it is no longer fragmented, it naturally expresses wholeness. And when it is no longer defended, it naturally reveals the depth that was always present beneath the noise of survival.

This is the felt sense of an awakened nervous system: a grounded presence that cannot be shaken by circumstance, a coherence that makes life feel like a single movement rather than scattered parts, and a depth that invites you into a life lived from the centre of your being rather than the edges of your defences. It is not a state you achieve; it is the body remembering how to exist without separation.

Absence of Inner Conflict

The absence of inner conflict is not a heroic achievement — it is what naturally emerges when the nervous system is no longer organized around fear. Inner conflict is, at its core, a physiological tension. It is the body tightening around a belief, resisting a sensation, or bracing against an emotion. When the survival system is activated, it generates competing impulses:

one part contracts to protect, another pushes toward change, another tries to suppress the contraction altogether. This fragmentation feels like “conflict,” but it is simply the body trying to manage too much perceived danger at once.

When the nervous system awakens, this fragmentation dissolves. You no longer feel pulled in multiple directions because there is no longer a part of you trying to control what you feel. Experience is no longer divided into what is welcome and what must be resisted. Everything arising in the inner world has space to move without being met by an opposing force. This is the ending of inner conflict — not through mental mastery, but through physiological coherence.

Without conflict, there is an unmistakable sense of ease. Decisions stop feeling like battles, for there is no internal opponent demanding certainty or safety. Emotions arise cleanly, move cleanly, and complete themselves without leaving behind the residue of self-judgment. Thoughts appear like ripples on a still lake rather than storms tearing through a fragile system. Even the mind’s old habits of doubt and worry lose their impact because the body is no longer reacting to them as if they pose danger.

This absence of conflict does not mean that challenges disappear. It means that challenges no longer activate the survival structure within you. You meet life without the old reflexive tightening. You respond rather than react. You move from clarity rather than tension. The body’s inner environment becomes so spacious and unresisted that even difficult sensations are experienced without the overlay of “should,” “shouldn’t,” “what if,” or “I can’t.” There is simply what arises, and the natural intelligence within you moves toward what is needed.

The most profound aspect of this absence of conflict is the silence it reveals. A silence not of emptiness, but of harmony. It is the silence of a system that is no longer fighting itself, no longer fragmenting consciousness into competing parts. It is the silence that comes when awareness and sensation are no longer in opposition. From that silence, life becomes simple — not because it is easy, but because nothing inside is resisting the truth of the moment.

In this way, the awakened nervous system becomes a sanctuary. You live inside yourself without fear. You inhabit your experience without dividing it. And in the absence of inner conflict, you discover a direct, unmediated connection to presence — a way of being in which every movement, every breath, every emotion arises within a seamless field of wholeness.

Ease in Sensation and Emotion

Ease in sensation and emotion does not arise because life becomes gentler, or because the body suddenly prefers pleasant experiences over difficult ones. It arises because the awakened nervous system no longer interprets what it feels as a threat. Sensation is allowed to be sensation. Emotion is allowed to be emotion. Nothing needs to be pushed away, controlled, managed, or transformed. The body is no longer bracing for impact, so whatever arises can simply move through without friction.

In an unawakened system, sensations often trigger stories, and stories create tension. A tight chest becomes “fear,” a heavy stomach becomes “danger,” a surge of energy becomes “something is wrong.” These interpretations activate the survival mechanism, contracting the body around what is felt. The discomfort is not in the sensation itself — it is in the resistance to it. Awakening dissolves this resistance. Sensations no longer escalate into narratives, and emotions no longer cascade into identity. They are experienced directly, free of the overlays that once amplified them into struggle.

As the body becomes more open, sensations begin to feel spacious rather than overwhelming. You may feel intensity, but not distress. You may feel deep emotion, but without drowning in it. The nervous system stops collapsing into old patterns because it has learned, through presence, that experience is safe. Even powerful emotions like grief, anger, or longing can be met with a tenderness that was previously unavailable. They reveal themselves as movements of energy, not threats to the self.

This ease is felt not as numbness or detachment, but as intimacy. You meet your inner world without flinching. You allow each wave to rise, crest, and fall, trusting the intelligence within the sensation itself. Emotions become doorways rather than obstacles — pathways into deeper contact with life. And because the system is no longer fighting them, they resolve naturally, sometimes within moments. The body no longer traps emotional energy in contractions; it metabolizes it into clarity.

Over time, this ease becomes a new baseline. You move through the world with a body that is permeable rather than armoured — able to feel without losing itself, able to open without collapsing, able to receive without closing. The emotional landscape becomes fluid, coherent, and trustworthy. You do not have to “manage” emotional states, because they are no longer destabilizing. They arise within a field of presence that is larger than any single feeling.

This is one of the quiet miracles of the awakened nervous system: your capacity to feel expands infinitely, but your suffering diminishes. The more you allow, the less you struggle. The more you feel, the freer you become. Sensation turns into guidance, emotion into movement, and the entire inner world shifts from something to control into something to lovingly experience. The body remembers that it was never meant to guard against life — it was meant to feel life fully, openly, and without fear.

The End of Ego Reactivity

The end of ego reactivity is not the disappearance of the ego — it is the disappearance of the contracted physiology that once *gave* the ego its urgency, its defensiveness, and its sense of threat. Reactivity has never been a psychological fault. It has always been a somatic response: the body tightening before the mind interprets, the nervous system bracing before the story forms. What we call "reactivity" is simply the survival system trying to protect the self it believes is at risk.

When the nervous system awakens, reactivity dissolves because the perceived threat dissolves. The system no longer interprets sensation, emotion, or external events as danger. There is no spike of cortisol, no rush of tightening, no internal scramble to defend a fragile identity. Instead, there is spaciousness around experience, a latency in which awareness has room to meet the moment before old patterns can activate. In this space, the ego loses the physiological fuel that once drove its reactions.

Egoic patterns may still arise — habits of thought, memories of old roles, ideas about who you are — but they do not capture you. They move through like echoes, unable to recruit the body into contraction. Without the body participating, the ego cannot solidify into a reactive identity. It becomes transparent, a movement within awareness rather than something you become. And because you no longer collapse into it, it has no ability to dictate your behaviour or distort your perception.

Reactivity ends not through suppression, discipline, or heightened self-control, but through the nervous system's profound shift from protection to openness. You feel an old emotional trigger rising, and instead of tightening, you soften. Instead of preparing for conflict, you remain present. Instead of collapsing into defence, you allow sensation to move freely. The very patterns that once controlled you now arise and dissolve within a larger field of coherence.

What emerges is clarity — not the sharp, brittle clarity of the mind trying to stay ahead of danger, but the clarity that comes from having nothing inside to defend. You respond to life without the residue of old wounds or the distortions of unconscious fear. Your actions become clean, direct, grounded in presence rather than driven by unintegrated emotion. People may still project onto you, misunderstand you, or challenge you, but nothing inside you flinches in response. You meet others without collapsing into old roles or compensatory behaviours.

This is the quiet beauty of the awakened nervous system: the ego becomes optional. Its stories no longer bind you, its fears no longer shape you, and its reactivity no longer defines you. You relate to the world from the depth of who you truly are, not the contraction of who you once believed you needed to be. Reactivity fades, not because you learned to rise above life, but because your body now knows — fully and irrevocably — that it is safe to remain open within it.

The Body as a Vessel for Presence

When the nervous system awakens, the body stops functioning as a container for tension and becomes a vessel for presence. This shift is subtle yet profound. Instead of holding accumulated fear, unfinished emotions, and protective contractions, the body becomes transparent — no longer a barrier between awareness and experience, but the medium through which awareness expresses itself. Presence is no longer something you visit in brief moments of stillness; it saturates the body, infusing every movement, sensation, and interaction.

An awakened body does not perform presence. It *embodies* it. Presence radiates not from effort but from the absence of resistance. The muscles are not bracing, the breath is not guarded, and the emotional field is not defended. Without these layers of contraction, awareness flows through the body with the same ease that wind moves through an open field. You feel alive not as a separate self watching life, but as the very aliveness that life is moving through.

This embodiment changes the quality of your interactions. People can sense the difference before they understand it. Your presence becomes regulating, grounding, and clarifying — not because you try to offer healing, but because the coherence within you naturally influences the systems around you. A body free of survival tension transmits safety. A body free of egoic urgency transmits openness. A body resting in awareness transmits truth without speaking a word. You become, simply by being, a field in which others can settle.

In this state, the body becomes exquisitely sensitive while remaining unwaveringly stable. Sensation deepens but does not destabilize. Emotions move freely but do not fragment. The body becomes spacious enough for all of human experience to arise without contraction, yet rooted enough for awareness to remain undisturbed. You inhabit yourself fully — every breath, every pulse, every subtle vibration — because nothing inside recoils from the fullness of aliveness.

The body as a vessel for presence is the culmination of the somatic path. It is the realization that awakening is not an escape from the physical form, but its fulfillment. The same body that once held separation becomes the living expression of unity. Sensation that once triggered fear now reveals depth. Emotions that once overwhelmed now open pathways into greater intimacy with life. The physical form that once seemed to limit you now becomes the very place where the infinite is known directly.

This is the awakened nervous system: a body no longer shaped by the past, no longer constricted by survival, no longer distorting experience through fear. It becomes a clear channel for presence — a living, breathing expression of awareness appearing as form. Through it, life flows unhindered, and you come to recognize that the body was never the obstacle to awakening. It was the doorway, the bridge, and ultimately the vessel through which awakening becomes real in the world.

The Nervous System Returned to Its Original Innocence

The awakened nervous system is not a new achievement but a homecoming. It is the body remembering its original innocence — the effortless openness that existed before fear reshaped it, before contraction became identity, before survival veiled the truth of what you are. In this return, the body no longer stands between you and awareness; it becomes the living expression of awareness itself.

What you discover is a physiology that no longer braces against life but moves with it. A system once fragmented by fear becomes coherent, stable, and deeply rooted in presence. Sensations that once overwhelmed now reveal depth. Emotions that once hijacked identity now move through with clarity. The old reflexes of reactivity dissolve, not by force, but by the nervous system's recognition that it is finally safe to release its grip.

This is the quiet revolution of embodiment: nothing inside you is at war anymore. The subtle conflict between mind and body, between emotion and identity, between awareness and sensation — dissolves. In its place arises a profound internal unity, a wholeness that cannot be manufactured through thought or effort. It comes only through the softening of the physiological structures that once held separation in place.

With this unity, presence becomes the way you live rather than a moment you seek. The body becomes the vessel through which clarity moves, intimacy deepens, and life expresses itself without distortion. You begin to experience yourself not as someone *trying* to awaken, but as the field of awareness that is already awake, already here, already infused into every breath, every sensation, every movement of life.

The awakened nervous system reveals a truth that the mind cannot grasp: awakening is not an escape from the human experience but the full inhabiting of it. It is the merging of depth and aliveness, stillness and sensation, clarity and form. It is the recognition that the body — once misunderstood as the obstacle — is the very ground through which awakening becomes real, embodied, and lived.

In this remembrance, nothing needs to be added, repaired, or perfected. The body has simply returned to its natural state: open, unguarded, coherent, and free. And from this freedom, you step into life not as someone navigating separation, but as the presence through which separation has dissolved.

Chapter

17

Embodying Stillness in Motion

Action Without Force

Action without force is the natural movement that arises when the nervous system is no longer bracing against life. It is not a strategy, not a technique, and not a posture of effort. It is the way life moves when nothing inside is tightening in anticipation of harm. In this sense, action becomes an expression of stillness — not because the body is inert, but because nothing within you is pushing, resisting, or compensating. What acts is not the conditioned self, but the spaciousness that remains when contraction has dissolved.

When action is rooted in force, it carries the unmistakable texture of separation. The body tightens, the breath narrows, and the movement forward is an attempt to secure something imagined to be missing. Even the most outwardly successful effort is burdened by an inner strain, as though you must continually prove, protect, or maintain the self you believe you are. Force is always an attempt to stabilize a threatened identity. Action without force, however, does not originate from identity at all. It emerges from the open awareness beneath it — an awareness that has no need to prove anything, because nothing is separate from it.

The more the body softens, the more you discover that action can arise effortlessly, like a current moving through you rather than something you generate. There is a sense of being carried by a deeper intelligence that does not require analysis or tension. You find yourself doing what needs to be done without the inner noise of self-judgment or self-reference. The movement flows, and you are simply its instrument. In this way, action begins to feel like listening — each step a response to life rather than an attempt to control it.

This kind of action is not passive. It is immensely potent, but its potency comes from clarity rather than pressure. When nothing in you is resisting the moment, your energy is no longer fragmented by fear or divided by doubt. The whole of your being becomes available to what is here. Effortless action is the expression of coherence — mind, heart, and body aligned not because you forced them to be, but because there is no longer a split between them.

To act without force is to move from the same stillness that underlies awakening itself. It is the recognition that doing does not have to take you away from presence. In fact, when the body is no longer tightening around a separate self, action becomes one of the purest expressions of presence. Every movement originates from the silence within you, and every step carries the imprint of that silence into form. You are no longer acting *to become* something; you act because life moves through you.

Here, action becomes spacious. Decisions arise with a natural ease. The body participates without tension. There is no sense of pushing the river, only moving with its current. And in this movement, you discover a profound truth: the stillness you once sought in meditation is not separate from the life you are living. It comes with you into motion. It breathes through you as you speak, walk, create, and respond.

This is the essence of action without force — the living demonstration that stillness is not the absence of movement, but the absence of resistance within movement. It is the beginning of discovering how awakening expresses itself through the body, not in retreat from the world, but in the very heart of participation.

Presence While Living

Presence while living is the realization that awakening is not an event reserved for quiet spaces, ideal conditions, or moments of deliberate practice. It is the capacity to remain in direct contact with reality as it unfolds — breath by breath, sensation by sensation — without abandoning yourself to the momentum of old patterns. Presence becomes less of a state you enter and more of a natural atmosphere you inhabit, an inner spaciousness that walks with you into every interaction, decision, and movement of daily life.

Most people know presence only in contrast to activity. They feel present while meditating, walking in nature, or sitting in silence — but the moment life accelerates, presence seems to dissolve. Yet what actually dissolves is not presence, but the fragile self that depends on ideal conditions to feel centred. True presence reveals itself not in the absence of movement, but in the midst of it. It is the quiet within the noise, the stillness beneath the motion, the spaciousness that does not disappear just because life becomes complex or demanding.

As the nervous system awakens and the inner contractions that once defined identity begin to soften, presence becomes more stable. It is no longer something you hold onto with effort; it is something you relax into. The body becomes less reactive, less threatened by intensity, and less compelled to escape into thought. In this openness, you discover that presence is not a fragile state that must be protected — it is the natural condition of an unburdened system. It is what remains when you are no longer tightening around a story of self.

Presence while living is not a performance. It does not require you to move slowly, speak softly, or adopt any particular spiritual persona. Presence is simply the felt recognition that you are here — that your awareness is not lost inside thought, not contracted around fear, not scattered through anticipation. You are inhabiting this moment fully, allowing it to shape you as much as you shape it. Life becomes intimate, textured, immediate. Even mundane tasks — washing dishes, driving, preparing food — are infused with a quiet aliveness.

What makes presence transformative is that it changes the quality of your participation in life. When you are present, you listen differently. You respond instead of react. You sense what is true rather than what is habitual. There is a natural compassion in your interactions, not because you are trying to be compassionate, but because presence dissolves the layers of self-protection that once stood between you and others. Presence makes you porous to life. It allows every moment to be felt directly rather than filtered through old conditioning.

To live from presence is to trust the intelligence that moves through you when you are not contracting. It is the recognition that your deepest clarity is available in real time, not only in hindsight. Presence becomes the bridge between awakening and action, between inner stillness and outer participation. You discover that you can be fully engaged in life without leaving yourself — without abandoning the quiet awareness that has been with you all along.

Ultimately, presence while living is the lived expression of unity. It is the recognition that nothing you encounter — no emotion, no conversation, no challenge — is separate from the awareness experiencing it. In this recognition, life becomes less of a series of events to manage and more of a continuous unfolding to meet. Presence becomes both your anchor and your expression, allowing you to move through the world with an ease that is not passive, but deeply alive.

Openness in Relationship

Openness in relationship is the lived expression of awakening in the space between two people. It is where the nervous system's unfolding meets the real-world intimacy of human connection — where the softened body, the unarmored heart, and the quiet spaciousness of awareness begin to participate in relationship without returning to old survival patterns. In this space, you discover that relationship is not something you *do*; it is something that emerges naturally when you no longer organize yourself around protection.

Most people approach relationship from a partially contracted state. Even in love, there is bracing — an unconscious tightening in the body that anticipates rejection, loss, misunderstanding, or the need to negotiate identity. These subtle contractions shape how we listen, how we speak, and how deeply we allow ourselves to be seen. The ego relates through tension because it believes relationship is a place of potential danger. But as the body awakens and old structures soften, a profound shift occurs: openness becomes safer than defence.

Openness in relationship does not mean collapsing boundaries or losing discernment. It means allowing the heart to remain unguarded without abandoning your own clarity. It is the freedom to stay present with another's experience while also staying rooted in your own. In this openness, the body no longer interprets closeness as a threat. It becomes a channel — transparent, receptive, unburdened. Your presence communicates more than your words ever could, and others feel held not by effort, but by the natural coherence of your being.

The remarkable thing about embodied openness is that it dissolves the illusion of separation not by merging identities, but by revealing the spaciousness in which both identities arise. You begin to sense the other not from your mind, but from the quiet depth of your own awareness. You listen without preparing your response. You receive without tightening. You allow the moment to shape you both. Relationship becomes less about managing dynamics and more about participating in a shared field of presence.

In this field, defensiveness softens. Misunderstandings resolve more quickly. Vulnerability no longer feels like exposure but like truth. You begin to discover that connection deepens not through perfect communication but through your willingness to remain open when every conditioned part of you wants to close. This is where relationship becomes sacred — a mirror in which you continually see where contraction remains, and an invitation into greater spaciousness each time you choose softness over self-protection.

Awakened openness in relationship is not an achievement; it is a natural outcome of an unburdened nervous system. When the body no longer carries the weight of survival, it naturally offers warmth, clarity, and attunement. It becomes easier to love, easier to forgive, easier to remain present in discomfort. Relationship becomes less of a negotiation and more of a mutual unfolding — two beings meeting without the distortions of past wounds.

Ultimately, openness in relationship is the recognition that the space between you and another is not a boundary but a bridge. It is where awakening reveals its tenderness, where presence becomes relational, where the dissolving of separation extends beyond your internal world and into the hearts of those around you. Through this openness, relationship becomes not a distraction from awakening but one of its clearest expressions — a living field where stillness moves, breathes, and becomes intimacy.

Grace in Challenge

Grace in challenge is the embodied recognition that difficulty does not have to collapse you back into the old patterns of fear, tightening, or self-defence. It is not the absence of challenge, nor the denial of discomfort, but the capacity to remain open while life intensifies. As the nervous system awakens and the body learns to soften rather than brace, challenge becomes less of an adversary and more of a doorway — an invitation into deeper presence, deeper truth, and deeper trust.

Grace arises when the inner ground is no longer organized around survival. In the past, challenge triggered the physiology of danger: the chest tightened, breath shortened, awareness narrowed. The body reflexively attempted to escape, fix, or control. Yet as awakening deepens, you begin to experience a subtle but profound shift. The body no longer interprets intensity as a threat. Instead of contracting, it allows. Instead of resisting, it receives. Instead of collapsing inward, it expands into a wider field of awareness that can hold the moment.

Grace is this expansion — this willingness to meet what is happening without running from it. In grace, you are no longer negotiating reality from fear. You are allowing it to move through you, trusting that your openness is stronger than any challenge that arises. Even when the mind doesn't know what to do, the deeper intelligence of your being remains steady. You feel yourself anchored not in certainty, but in presence. And this presence gives rise to responses that are clearer, kinder, and more aligned than anything constructed from tension.

Grace in challenge does not mean you float above your life untouched. You still feel emotions, still encounter difficulty, still experience the rawness of being human. But your relationship to these experiences has transformed. Sensations move through you without becoming identity. Emotions arise without becoming self. Even shock or pain does not tear you away from yourself; it simply moves through the spaciousness you now inhabit. Grace is not found in bypassing sensation — it is found in staying with it without closing.

Interestingly, challenge often reveals the depth of your awakening more clearly than peace ever could. When everything is easy, it is simple to feel spacious. But when life tests the edges of your capacity, you discover how much contraction still remains — and how much awareness has already taken root. Each moment of challenge becomes a mirror: will you return to the old shell of self-protection, or will you let this moment widen you further?

Grace grows whenever you choose openness. And each time you choose openness in the midst of intensity, something within you reorganizes. The nervous system learns that it no longer needs to collapse around fear. The heart learns that it can stay open even when vulnerable. Awareness learns that nothing arising within it has the power to destabilize it. Through this, challenge becomes the very terrain in which awakening matures.

Ultimately, grace in challenge is the lived expression of a deeper truth: life is not happening *to* you but *through* you. The waves may rise, but the ocean of your being remains unchanged. When this is known not intellectually but somatically, challenge becomes another movement of the same life that breathes you. And in that realization, grace is inevitable — a natural radiance of openness meeting the world exactly as it is.

Awakening Lived Through the Body

Awakening lived through the body is the moment when spirituality ceases to be an inner experience and becomes the very atmosphere of your life. It is when awakening is no longer something you *touch* in meditation or glimpse in moments of clarity, but something that expresses itself through your movements, your choices, your relationships, your presence, and the way your nervous system meets the world. The body, once shaped by contraction and conditioned to defend a separate self, becomes the living conduit through which unity moves.

In the early stages of awakening, the body often feels like the last place where separation dissolves. Patterns of fear, bracing, and emotional residue linger, pulling you back into familiar identity. But as the somatic work deepens — through softening, releasing, and allowing — something extraordinary occurs: the body no longer protects you from life, it participates in life as life. Your physiology aligns with truth. Your breath aligns with openness. Your posture aligns with what is uncontrived and natural. Awakening becomes less of a state and more of a full-body coherence.

When awakening is lived through the body, you no longer feel like awareness *visiting* the body; you feel like awareness *inhabiting* it. Sensation becomes a companion rather than a problem to solve. Emotion becomes movement rather than identity. Experience arises and passes through without interruption, because nothing in you is grasping, resisting, or tightening around it. The body becomes porous — transparent to the moment, receptive to the flow of life, free from the reflexive contraction that once shaped your sense of self.

Action becomes an effortless extension of this embodied spaciousness. You move when movement arises, speak when words form naturally, and rest when the body calls for stillness. There is no inner argument. No division between what you know and what you do. The body, once the source of confusion and reactivity, now becomes the instrument of clear expression. It is the bridge between the vastness of your inner awareness and the tangible world in which you live.

To live awakening through the body is to rediscover simplicity. You do not need to manage every thought or monitor every reaction. The nervous system itself — once burdened by survival — has learned to return to openness as its baseline. This openness expresses as kindness without effort, clarity without strain, intimacy without fear. People feel this in you before you say a word. Your presence becomes transmission, not by intention but by ease.

Even challenges do not pull you out of this embodied awakening; they deepen it. The body meets difficulty not by collapsing but by softening, not by resisting but by expanding. Experience becomes an ally in your unfolding rather than an obstacle to your peace. Awakening is no longer something you protect; it is something you trust. It is no longer fragile; it is lived.

Ultimately, awakening lived through the body is the fulfillment of the path. It is the moment when the inner truth of oneness expresses effortlessly through the form you inhabit. You move through the world not as someone trying to stay awake, but as someone for whom wakefulness is the natural state. The body becomes a vessel of stillness in motion, a living expression of the unity that has always been here. Through this embodiment, awakening ceases to be an experience and becomes a way of being — quiet, grounded, luminous, and profoundly human.

The Body Becomes the Path, the Movement, and the Mirror

In the end, embodying stillness in motion reveals a truth so simple it is easily overlooked: awakening is never separate from the life you are living. It does not wait for you in meditation, nor hide in some elevated state beyond ordinary experience. It unfolds — in real time — through the body that breathes, feels, moves, and meets the world each day. What once seemed like two paths — inner stillness and outer action — are discovered to be a single, continuous expression of the same awareness.

The deeper you travel into the somatic dimensions of awakening, the more you realize that the body is not an obstacle to presence but the very field where presence becomes real. It is here, in the subtle dissolving of contraction and the quiet softening of old defences, that awakening roots itself in something stable and lived. Stillness ceases to be a state you chase and becomes the ground from which life effortlessly arises. Motion ceases to be a distraction and becomes the movement of that stillness into form.

Every challenge becomes an invitation into greater openness. Every relationship becomes a mirror that reveals where love wants to expand. Every action becomes a way that awareness learns to express itself through your form. And the body — once organized around survival — now becomes a vessel capable of transmitting clarity, safety, and alignment simply through its way of being.

This chapter marks a turning point in the journey: from awakening as an inner transformation to awakening as embodied participation. You are no longer learning how to bring presence into your life; presence *is* the life you are living. Stillness is not something you retreat into, but something you carry with you — into motion, into relationship, into challenge, into creation.

And as this integration deepens, something profound becomes unmistakable: your body becomes not only the path to awakening, but the instrument through which awakening touches the world. The separation between inner truth and outer expression dissolves. What remains is a life lived from coherence, a nervous system attuned to openness, and a presence that moves with grace through every unfolding moment.

In this way, the awakened body becomes a quiet blessing — a living reminder that oneness is not a destination, but the nature of everything you are and everything you meet.

Chapter

18

The Body as an Expression of Source

Identity Dissolves Into Awareness

As awakening deepens through the body, something subtle yet undeniable begins to shift: the one who believed themselves to be at the centre of experience starts to thin out, soften, and eventually dissolve into the very awareness that has always held them. What once felt like "me" — a constellation of memories, tensions, reactions, and meanings — loses its solidity, not through effort but through the simple recognition that it was never anything more than sensation shaped into a story. Identity unravels not because it is pushed away, but because the body is no longer bracing to protect it.

The nervous system, once organized around survival and separation, begins to express a different intelligence. In the softening of contraction, in the willingness to feel without gripping, a deeper truth reveals itself: awareness was never inside the identity. Identity was arising inside awareness. This shift is not philosophical but somatic — an unguarded exhale, a loosening in the chest, a widening in the internal space where experience is allowed to move freely. The ego, once felt as tightness or readiness or vigilance, is sensed now as a pattern of energy dissipating into something infinitely more spacious.

As identification releases, the body no longer serves as the container for a separate self but as a living expression of the field in which all things arise. Sensation becomes less personal. Emotion loses its narrative gravity. Even thought appears like weather passing through an open sky, no longer claiming ownership or demanding allegiance. The centre that once felt like "I" dissolves, not into emptiness but into immediacy — a directness of being that needs no definition.

In this unfolding, awareness and the body cease to be experienced as two. The body becomes transparency itself, a conduit through which the movement of Source can be felt without distortion. What remains is not a refined identity but the natural vibrancy of existence moving effortlessly through form. You do not witness life; you *are* life, aware of itself through this human expression. And in this recognition, the last refuge of separation falls away. There is no longer "me" experiencing the moment — there is only the moment, awake to itself, breathing itself into being through the body that once believed it was the doer.

This is the somatic completion of identity: not its eradication, but its return to the field from which it emerged. Awareness is no longer something you access — it is what you are. And the body, freed from the burden of holding a self, becomes the shimmering doorway through which that truth is lived.

Sensation Becomes Sacred

As identity dissolves into the field of awareness, something extraordinary and profoundly simple reveals itself: sensation — once interpreted, managed, resisted, or used to reinforce a sense of self — becomes undeniably sacred. What was previously dismissed as “just the body,” or endured as discomfort, or clung to as pleasure, is now recognized as the living pulse of Source expressing through form. Every flicker of sensation becomes an intimate meeting with reality as it is, free of the filters that once distorted it.

Sensation is no longer a problem to solve or an experience to regulate; it becomes the language of the infinite speaking through the finite. A subtle warmth in the chest, a gentle vibration along the spine, a soft expansion behind the heart — these are no longer merely “bodily states.” They are doorways, invitations into the immediacy of presence. Even what once felt dense or difficult reveals itself as nothing more than energy shifting its configuration, seeking freedom through awareness. With no identity grasping at meaning, sensation returns to its original purity.

The sacredness emerges not from the sensation itself, but from the space in which it is felt. Awareness no longer contracts around the experience. Instead, it receives sensation with the same openness it would give to a sunrise or a breath of wind. The body becomes a temple — not because it is ideal or perfected, but because it is finally recognized as an instrument for experiencing the divine in motion. Sensation and awareness weave together into a single tapestry, seamless and unbroken.

In this state, the entire sensory world becomes luminous. Touch carries a kind of holiness, as though each contact reveals an unseen dimension of aliveness. The beat of the heart feels like a mantra spoken from within. The breath becomes a prayer, not recited but enacted. Even stillness is alive — vibrating, humming, shimmering with the subtle intelligence that animates all of existence. Nothing is ordinary; everything is infused with presence.

And so, the body is no longer experienced as something you inhabit or observe. It becomes a living field of sacred sensation, a direct expression of consciousness knowing itself. Each moment of feeling becomes a portal into unity, a reminder that nothing in this human form is separate from the vastness that holds it. The sacred is no longer something sought beyond the body — it is felt, continuously, as the body's true nature unveiled.

Life Expresses Through the Awakened Form

When identity releases into awareness and sensation is reclaimed as sacred, the body itself becomes an unobstructed channel for the movement of life. What once felt personal — your impulses, your choices, your gestures, your desires — now reveals itself as the effortless expressing of Source through a human form no longer burdened by contraction. Action arises without friction. Decisions emerge without inner argument. Life begins to flow through you with the same naturalness with which wind moves through an open field.

In this state, nothing is manufactured from effort. There is no attempt to manage the moment or control the unfolding. Instead, the body responds to life like a finely tuned instrument — sensitive, receptive, coherent. The nervous system no longer organizes itself around protecting a self-image or avoiding sensation; it organizes around truth. Movement arises as intelligence rather than strategy. Words come from clarity rather than identity. Even stillness has its own expression, not as withdrawal but as radiant presence.

What becomes unmistakable is that *you are not doing life*. Life is doing you — expressing, breathing, creating through your form. This does not diminish agency; it purifies it. Agency becomes participation rather than control, alignment rather than effort. Choices are no longer weighed from fear or habit but felt as the next natural movement of the whole. You find yourself saying yes more easily, no more cleanly, and moving through the world with a kind of quiet precision that was impossible when the ego was steering.

The awakened form becomes a mirror through which others feel their own possibility. Your body communicates coherence without speaking. Your presence regulates without intention. Your openness invites openness. The intelligence that moves through you is not personal wisdom but the rhythm of the universe expressed at a human scale. You become a living reminder that awakening is not an escape from the body but its fulfillment — life fully inhabiting its creation.

As this embodiment stabilizes, even the ordinary becomes luminous. Eating, walking, communicating, working — each becomes an extension of wholeness expressing itself in unique detail. Nothing is separate from the field of awareness that animates it. There is no distinction between the sacred and the mundane; all of it reveals the same Source moving through the same open form.

In this way, the awakened body becomes life's instrument — transparent, available, responsive. The boundary between "self" and "life" dissolves, leaving only the seamless flow of being expressing itself through human shape. And in this transparency, you discover the quiet miracle that was always present: existence has always been living through you, waiting only for the space to reveal itself.

Unity as the Only Remaining Truth

As the awakened body becomes a transparent expression of life, the final illusion quietly dissolves — the belief that anything stands apart from anything else. Unity is no longer an idea glimpsed in moments of insight; it becomes the undeniable ground of experience. What once felt like "inner" and "outer," "self" and "other," "form" and "spirit," merges into a single field of living presence. The body, freed from defending an identity, reveals what it had been pointing to all along: there is only one movement, one intelligence, one awareness appearing as the many.

In this recognition, separation is seen as a temporary posture the nervous system once adopted for survival, not a truth about reality. Every contraction that once shaped identity, every emotional imprint that once narrowed perception, every survival reflex that once made life feel divided — all of it unravels into the same spacious knowing. Unity is not achieved; it is uncovered, like the sky revealed when clouds disperse. It was always here, waiting for the body to stop bracing against life.

What remains is a clarity so simple it defies the mind's attempts to understand it: everything arises *as* you because everything arises *in* you. Not the personal "you," but the vast field of awareness that the body now expresses without distortion. The wind moving across your skin is not separate from the consciousness that feels it. The person before you is not separate from the presence that recognizes them. Even the sensations within your own body are no longer experienced as "mine," but as the shimmering play of the same unified field taking shape for a moment.

Unity becomes the only remaining truth because nothing in your lived experience contradicts it anymore. The body no longer tightens around preference, fear, or identity. The heart no longer closes in protection. Awareness no longer collapses into thought. Every gesture, every breath, every feeling arises from the same indivisible whole. Life is not happening *to* you; life is happening *as* you, through you, around you, within the same continuous field.

This unity does not erase the uniqueness of your form — it illuminates it. Your expression becomes one facet of the infinite reflecting itself, one flowering of a consciousness that never begins and never ends. The human experience becomes a celebration of diversity within oneness, movement within stillness, form within the boundless.

And in this realization, peace becomes effortless. Not because life becomes perfect, but because the one who resisted life is no longer present. Only unity remains — quiet, luminous, all-encompassing. A truth so intimate it can only be lived through the body, breathed moment by moment, as awakening finally completes its descent into form.

The Somatic Completion of Awakening

The final movement of awakening does not occur in the mind, nor in insight, nor even in expanded states of consciousness. It completes itself in the body — quietly, steadily, inevitably — as the last traces of separation melt from the nervous system. Awakening is no longer something understood, glimpsed, or visited; it becomes the natural condition of your lived experience. The body, once shaped by contraction and survival, now becomes an unguarded instrument of presence, effortlessly expressing the unity that has always been true.

In this completion, nothing needs to be transcended. Nothing needs to be fixed. Nothing needs to be purified or improved. Instead, the body is reclaimed as the place where consciousness lands fully — where awareness is not hovering above experience but saturating it, breathing through it, animating it. The densest sensations, the most vulnerable emotions, the subtle vibrational currents that move through the tissues all become part of awakening rather than obstacles to it. Nothing is excluded from the field; therefore, nothing is left outside of love.

You realize that the journey was never about rising above the human experience but about descending fully into it without resistance. The nervous system, once conditioned to brace against life, now trusts life so completely that openness is the default state. Even when intensity arises, it moves freely. Even when emotion surfaces, it does not contract into identity. The somatic field becomes fluid, permeable, transparent — no longer shaping a self, but reflecting the seamlessness of awareness.

In this transparency, there is a sense of profound simplicity. The searching stops because the seeker has dissolved. The striving ends because there is no longer anything to attain. Life unfolds without the interference of an internal commentary trying to direct it. Presence becomes embodied to the point that there is no distinction between being aware and being alive — they merge into one unbroken movement. The body becomes the living proof that awakening is not an escape from form, but its fulfillment.

This somatic completion also brings a depth of compassion that is almost indescribable. Because nothing within you is held apart, nothing outside you feels separate. You meet others with the same openness your body now extends to all sensation. Your presence becomes a quiet invitation for others to soften into their own truth. There is no effort to teach or influence; the transmission is simply your state of being.

Ultimately, the somatic completion of awakening is the recognition that the body itself was never a barrier — it was the path. It was the doorway through which awareness remembered itself, the vessel through which unity entered form, the ground upon which the illusion of separation finally dissolved. And now, what remains is life living itself through you with nothing in the way — pure, effortless, complete.

The Human Form as Divine Transparency

As this final movement of the journey unfolds, the truth becomes unmistakable: the body was never a limitation, never an obstacle, never something to transcend. It was the very place where awakening awaited you. Through every contraction released, every sensation welcomed, every layer of identity softened, the body gradually revealed its true nature — not as the seat of a separate self, but as the luminous transparency through which Source expresses itself in form.

What you once called "my body" is now experienced as a living field of awareness, shaped into human contours but belonging to the infinite. There is no longer a you inside it. There is only life moving, intelligence expressing, love unfolding in ways both subtle and profound. The distinction between presence and embodiment dissolves; awareness is not something you return to, but the continuous ground of your existence. The body simply lives from that ground with ease.

This is the quiet miracle of embodied awakening: the sacred and the ordinary merge until they are indistinguishable. Eating, speaking, resting, relating — each becomes an expression of the same unified field. Nothing is performed; everything is revealed. The awakened form becomes an open conduit for the timeless to touch the world, not through grand gestures but through the simplicity of being fully here.

And so, the journey resolves itself not in transcendence, but in intimacy with what is. In the fullness of sensation. In the transparency of identity. In the recognition that unity was never something to reach but something to remember through the body. What remains is a life lived from wholeness — effortless, coherent, and profoundly free.

The body, once carrying the weight of separation, now stands as a testament to what becomes possible when consciousness descends fully into form. You become not someone awakened, but the awakening itself — the living bridge between the unbounded Source and the world it animates. This is the completion of the path and the beginning of a different kind of life: one where nothing stands between you and the infinite that moves through you.

Epilogue: The Remembering of Oneness

What Awakening Now Means

Awakening, as it unfolds in this time and in this human body, is no longer the mythic escape from form that many once imagined. It is not the disappearance of the self into some distant transcendence, nor the attainment of a state that removes you from the world. Awakening now is the quiet, unequivocal recognition that the very ground of your experience — your breath, your sensation, your heartbeat, your relationships, your emotions — is not separate from the vastness you once sought. It is the remembrance that the Source you longed to touch has always been touching you from the inside.

To awaken now is to discover that nothing needs to be abandoned for truth to be known. Instead, everything is seen as an expression of truth. The body, once felt as an obstacle, becomes the intimate doorway. Sensation, once feared or resisted, becomes the living language of presence. Emotion becomes movement within awareness. Experience stops being something you manage and becomes something you meet.

Awakening now is the dissolving of the imagined boundary between the one who witnesses and what is witnessed. The distance collapses. The line softens. The world is no longer "out there" and you are no longer "in here." There is just one continuous field of being, appearing as breath, as sensation, as relationship, as life moving through the form you inhabit.

It is a shift from striving to recognition, from seeking to allowing, from effort to transparency. Not because you have transcended your humanity, but because your humanity has been reclaimed by the truth of what you are. Awakening now is inherently embodied — because there is nowhere else for it to land. The mind may understand unity, but the body remembers it.

And in this remembering, awakening becomes less an event and more a way of being. A softness in the system. A permeability. A willingness to experience life directly, without tightening around it. The awakened state is not separate from ordinary existence; it reveals the sacredness woven into the ordinary.

Awakening now means living as the openness that you once believed you needed to reach. It means recognizing that you were never moving toward oneness — you were dissolving the contractions that hid the fact that you were never anything else. It is the return to a truth that has never changed, experienced through a body that is finally ready to feel it.

The Return to Your Natural State

The return to your natural state is not a forward movement but a falling back — an undoing, a softening, a remembering of what has always been here beneath the layers of survival and self-protection. It is the recognition that the ease, openness, and coherence you have touched throughout this journey were never achievements; they were glimpses of your original condition before contraction shaped itself into identity.

Your natural state is not something you cultivate. It emerges on its own when the body no longer needs to brace against life.

When the nervous system relaxes its vigilance, when sensation is allowed rather than managed, when emotion is met rather than resisted, the system reveals what has been true all along: you are already whole. You are already connected. You are already supported by something infinitely larger than the self you once defended.

This return is quiet. It does not announce itself with fireworks or grand spiritual events. It feels more like the exhale you didn't realize you were holding for years. A deep settling. A feeling of being at home within your own form. The world does not change, yet everything in your experience becomes softer, more permeable, more intimate. Life is no longer something happening to you; it is happening as you.

To return to your natural state is to rediscover the simplicity beneath the complexity — the stillness beneath the story, the spaciousness beneath the emotion, the awareness beneath the identity. It is a shift from efforting into alignment to noticing that alignment was never absent. It was only obscured by the nervous system's learned contraction.

And as the body remembers this naturalness, you begin to live in a way that is unforced. Choices arise from clarity rather than fear. Boundaries emerge from truth rather than tension. Love flows without needing permission. The movement of your life becomes coherent with the deeper currents of existence — not because you tried to become spiritual, but because you stopped interfering with what was always guiding you.

Your natural state is not a state you enter. It is the one you return to when separation dissolves. It is the effortless being you inhabited before the world taught your body to tighten. It is the innocence of awareness shining through form, once again unburdened.

This is the great paradox of awakening: the journey ends not in becoming more, but in becoming what you have always been. The return to your natural state is the return to yourself — not the self you constructed, but the self that existed before construction was ever necessary.

The Body's Final Role: Dissolving Separation

The body, which once appeared to be the source of separation, becomes in the end the very instrument through which separation dissolves. What was once experienced as limitation becomes the doorway to boundlessness. The contractions that shaped identity become invitations into spaciousness. The sensations you once feared become the pathways home.

This is the body's final role — not to transcend itself or disappear, but to reveal that it was never separate from the field of awareness in the first place. As the nervous system unwinds its ancient habits of defence, the body stops insisting on its own boundaries. It becomes porous, open, transparent to the deeper intelligence moving through it. Sensation loses its sharp edges. Emotion loses its narrative weight. Experience becomes less "mine" and more simply arising.

In this transparency, the body becomes a living testament to unity. It no longer organizes around fear, vigilance, or survival. It organizes around openness. It organizes around coherence. It organizes around truth. The body that once encoded the ego's division now expresses the simplicity of being itself.

Dissolving separation is not an abstract spiritual event; it is a physiological release. The final remnants of the ego's grip show up in the tissues, the breath, the micro-contractions that once held the world at a distance. As these soften, what remains is an intimate continuity with everything around you. You feel life directly — not as something you observe, but as something you are inseparable from.

In the end, the body does not awaken *to* oneness — it awakens *as* oneness. The boundary between awareness and form dissolves. You no longer inhabit the body as a separate self; the body becomes an expression of the same vastness that animates the trees, the wind, the sky, the breath of every being. There is no inner and outer, no self and other — just the effortless movement of existence through the shape you temporarily call "me."

The body's final role is simply this: to stop defending itself long enough for you to recognize the truth that has been here all along. When the last contraction melts, the last belief softens, the last identification loosens, there is no moment of triumph — only a gentle, undeniable knowing that nothing was ever separate.

In that moment, the body reveals its deepest offering: it becomes the bridge through which the illusion of separation fades, allowing the fullness of oneness to shine unobstructed through your human form.

Living as the Field, Not the Fragment

To live as the field rather than the fragment is to move through life no longer from the vantage point of a separate self, but from the unbroken wholeness that has always been here. It is not an achievement or a perfected state; it is the natural consequence of the body relaxing out of its lifelong contraction. When the grip of identity dissolves, what remains is a way of being that is spacious, inclusive, and deeply intimate with all of existence.

Living as the field means you no longer experience life through the narrow aperture of "me." Perception widens. Awareness softens. The boundary between your experience and the world becomes permeable, then indistinct, and finally irrelevant. You begin to sense that everything you encounter — every emotion, every sensation, every interaction — arises within the same seamless presence. Life is not happening to you or around you; it is happening through you, as you, and with you.

The fragment fights, defends, strategizes, and navigates. The field rests, responds, and expresses. The fragment seeks control; the field moves in coherence with what is. In the fragment, the world feels personal and often threatening. In the field, nothing is personal because everything is part of the same unfolding. The heart remains open not because circumstances warrant it, but because openness is no longer optional — it is simply what you are.

As the field, your choices arise from clarity rather than fear. Your presence affects others not by effort but by resonance. Your actions carry the quality of stillness even when they are dynamic. You become a stabilizing force in the world, not by doing anything special, but because your nervous system no longer broadcasts separation. People feel seen around you without needing to be understood. They feel safe without knowing why. They feel themselves without losing themselves.

Living as the field is the embodied realization that every moment is an expression of one life, one consciousness, one source moving through infinite forms. The body is no longer a container for a self — it is a channel for being. Relationship is no longer a meeting of two — it is awareness seeing itself from different angles. Experience is no longer evaluated — it is allowed.

There is a profound simplicity here. The field does not struggle to be spiritual or awakened or whole. It does not try to maintain a state. It does not fear losing itself. It simply exists in effortless coherence, allowing life to unfold with the same intelligence that moves galaxies and opens flowers.

This is the quiet fullness of living as the field: a life where nothing is outside of you, nothing is missing, nothing is defended, and nothing is separate. It is the recognition that the fragment was only ever a temporary lens — and the field is what you have always been.

A Closing Blessing on the Path of Embodiment

May this path return you to the simplicity that was always yours — the ease beneath the striving, the softness beneath the armour, the vastness beneath the name you took on to survive. May your body become the sanctuary it was meant to be, a place where nothing is exiled and nothing is forced, where sensation is welcomed as truth and emotion is honoured as movement.

May you trust the intelligence that breathes you, moves you, and holds you in every moment, even when the mind cannot understand. May you remember that awakening is not an ascent but a descent — a falling back into the depth of your own being, into the unbroken ground of awareness that has accompanied you through every contraction, every story, every forgetting.

May the parts of you that once braced against life feel the safety to release. May the places that once tightened around fear discover the quiet courage of openness. And may you come to know, not as a concept but as a lived reality, that nothing in you was ever separate from the Source that animates all things.

As you walk forward, may life meet you with the same gentleness you offer it. May your presence become a refuge — for yourself, for those you love, and for those who simply cross your path without knowing why they feel seen. May your body express the coherence of truth, your actions arise from clarity, and your relationships reveal the unity you now embody.

And above all, may you remember that this journey is not about becoming something new, but about unveiling what has always been here. You are not walking toward oneness — you are returning to the recognition that you were never anything else.

May this remembrance guide you, steady you, soften you, and illuminate your days. May it carry you into a life lived not from separation, but from the fullness of the field that you are.

The Quiet Return Home

In the end, awakening is not a grand event or a final summit reached — it is the quiet return home to what you have always been. It is the soft recognition that the journey, with all its shedding and unfolding, was never about becoming more awakened, but about removing what obscured the truth that lived beneath every breath.

All along, the body carried the map. Every contraction pointed toward what had not yet been met. Every tightening revealed where separation still lived. Every opening showed you what was possible when fear loosened its hold. Through each sensation, each release, each moment of presence, the body guided you back to the simplicity of being.

This remembering is not the end of something; it is the beginning of living from a deeper ground of awareness — one that does not waver with emotion or circumstance. It is the discovery that clarity can coexist with vulnerability, that openness can walk hand in hand with strength, that love is not something you practice but something that naturally expresses when the nervous system is no longer shaped by survival.

The remembering of oneness is not a state you must maintain. It is a truth that quietly permeates your life once the illusion of separation has softened. It reveals itself in the quality of your presence, in the ease of your choices, in the tenderness you extend toward yourself and others. It reveals itself each time you exhale into this moment and recognize that nothing is lacking.

You have not attained oneness — you have remembered it. You have not transcended the body — you have allowed it to become transparent to the vastness within. You have not erased the human experience — you have illuminated it with the light of awareness.

As this journey continues in your daily life, may you trust the simplicity of what you now know: that you are already whole, already held, already one with everything you meet.

Return to the body, again and again, whenever the mind forgets. This is the quiet return home. And from here, your life becomes the expression of that oneness — effortless, intimate, and profoundly free.

www.ingramcontent.com/pod-product-compliance
Lightning Source LLC
LaVergne TN
LVHW010646110826
845149LV00014B/2970

* 9 7 8 1 0 6 9 9 7 7 2 0 5 *